Wader -
Cavens

Love

Maxy

FROM THE RAJ
TO THE OLD RECTORY

FROM THE RAJ
TO THE OLD RECTORY

MAXINE MAGAN

MICHAEL RUSSELL

First published in Great Britain 2006
by Michael Russell (Publishing) Ltd
Wilby Hall, Wilby, Norwich NR16 2JP

Typeset in Sabon by Waveney Typesetters
Wymondham, Norfolk
Printed and bound in Great Britain
by Biddles Ltd, King's Lynn, Norfolk

ISBN 978-0-85955-302-5

Contents

Contents

Author's Note

I am very grateful to Sheila Alcock for her support and encouragement and to Michael Russell for what he calls bossiness and I call help. Most of the illustrations and a little of the text were taken from my privately circulated family record 'In the Service of Empire'.

I

The Creswells

It is never too late to start writing, I was assured by a well-known author when I was eighty-nine. Encouraged, I joined a small writing group in nearby Tunbridge Wells, who all wrote short stories. They liked my first offering and pressed me to set on record a life which had its family roots in Empire, knew the ways of Empire in both India and Africa, the exigencies of war, and then a new beginning in our erstwhile rectory in Kent.

I decided I should start the record from before I was born or even thought of. To guide me I had a very heavy box of family papers, with notes on my forebears and family over several centuries. Amongst them I found a letter from Charles Grant, Director of the East India Company, appointing the Revd William McKinnon Fraser, my great-great-great-grandfather (whose wife Margaret was a niece of Charles Grant), to a chaplaincy in Bengal. Margaret died when their daughter Mary was born. A packet of twelve frail and crumbling letters written four years later, in 1829, by William Fraser survives. I unfolded the twenty-nine small pages. He clings throughout to his Christian faith to support him through his 'Dark Valley'. He says, 'In all Trials, Sorrow enables us to seek consolation in Thy Mercy.'

I could hardly bear to continue deciphering the faded writing: his grief seemed to pervade every sentence. But he evidently rallied enough to marry again, this time to a Miss Way. His young daughter Mary did not get on with her stepmother and returned to Scotland to live with her grandparents, Parson Rory McKenzie and his wife Margaret of Knockbain in the Black Isle.

Parson Rory, Mary's grandfather, was an imposing figure, six foot tall, broad shouldered with bold features and a Highland twinkle in his eye. He always wore the kilt and was a first-rate shot, stalker, and the boon companion of every sportsman on the Black Isle. His capacity for whisky was phenomenal. He was called locally 'mon but no meenister'; the previous minister had been known as 'meenister but no mon'. This colourful background seems to have suited Mary; she was very happy living with her grandparents.

In 1842, when Mary was seventeen, her aunt, Annie Fraser, thought she needed a little more sophistication than could be provided in the small parish of Knockbain, and decided to take her, with two of her cousins, to learn some of the arts and graces to be experienced in the capitals of Europe. They travelled from Scotland by a P & O ship, enduring a very rough journey across the Bay of Biscay, and were thankful to arrive at the Port of Gibraltar. Here the vessel was met by the handsome young Edmund Creswell, in his role as packet agent. Mary Fraser, looking demure, was very attracted to Edmund and laughed at his jokes. (He was said to have had 'a marvellous sense of the ridiculous'.) Aunt Annie was shocked, and said Mary should never have laughed as she had not been introduced. Aunt Annie then found she had letters of introduction to Edmund's sister, Mrs Cowell, who came with Edmund to call on them at their hotel. There was a lot of fluttering upstairs as the girls hunted for their gloves (to conform with social niceties) but then Aunt Annie had to introduce Mary formally to both Harriet Cowell and Edmund.

Only a week after their arrival, the Frasers were invited to an afternoon dance on HMS *Malabar*. There Edmund proposed to Mary. She said she could not reply as her Aunt Annie would hear, but Edmund said he was sure she was deaf. In fact she was far from deaf, and strongly disapproved; but she had another setback when the local archdeacon and his wife recommended Edmund. Reluctantly, she had to agree to their engagement and they were permitted to write to each other. They were finally married in the English church in Florence in 1844. Edmund bought the wedding ring in one of the little gold working shops on the bridge over the Arno. And the initially disapproving Aunt Annie lived with them for the rest of her life.

Edmund Creswell was the second son of 'Exodus' Edmund, corn factor, of Ratham Mill near Lewes, who, probably due to the post-Napoleonic depression, had accepted the post of packet agent, Gibraltar, from Lord Chichester, Postmaster General of the day. Exodus Edmund hired a schooner and set sail for Gibraltar in 1822, with his wife and six of his seven children. The journey took six weeks, and the children said they had eaten the last ship's biscuit before they arrived.

Exodus Edmund sent his son Edmund to school in England – at the school founded by the family of Sir Rowland Hill, who was both a pupil and later headmaster before his rise to Penny Post fame. The school was established on the basis of boys disciplining themselves, but this was not a very long-lived experiment.

Edmund returned to Gibraltar at seventeen and set to work in the Military Secretary's office of the Gibraltar Garrison. His father died a year later, so at eighteen Edmund became the breadwinner for his mother Susannah and his family. There can have been no doubt as to his ability as he was immediately offered the post of packet agent in place of his father. He also became Secretary to the Governor and edited the *Gibraltar Chronicle*, which he later improved into a fine local newspaper. The packet agency was later amalgamated with the Post Office and Edmund was made Deputy Postmaster General and Surveyor of the British Post Offices in the Mediterranean. He used to travel to Malta, Corfu, Constantinople, Alexandria, Beirut, Port Said and Suez, as well as to many international conferences. He had always wanted to be a barrister, but as he had to earn money for the family, he had to be content with his current job.

His marriage to Mary seems to have been exceptionally happy. One of their daughters, Annie, wrote: 'Absolute love reigned always.' They had thirteen children, one of whom, Kate, was my father's mother. They lived at 'The Palace' which had style but was not as splendid as the name suggests. (The Governor of Gibraltar, conversely, lived in a house called 'The Cottage'). 'The Palace' had been built by Arengo, a Genoese merchant who victualled the garrison during the siege of Gibraltar in 1779–83 and was rewarded with a charter from George III to own land and build a house for himself. In later years it was turned into an officers' club.

The Creswells were also closely connected with the Carver family, of whom Humphrey Carver, government architect in Ottawa, writes in his book *The Gibraltar Connection*. I have a letter from Field Marshal Lord Carver (my cousin Michael) showing how we came to be cousins. He doesn't get it quite right: it shows just one of the Carver-Creswell connections but the relationship was more complicated than that, as the families intermarried six times in different generations.

The Creswell family spent the summer months at Campamento, a fishing village on the sea in Spain. Great-Uncle Willie (later Admiral Sir William Creswell), writes:

> I was the fourth of a very large family. My mother, Mary Margaret Ward, née Fraser, was one of the Balnain and Farraline branch of the Fraser clan, and traced her descent back to the main Lovat line in the sixteenth century. My childhood days were as happy as could be. It was an ideal life for us boys, with shooting and riding, fishing and bathing, and all the recreation an outdoor lad delights in. The summer months we spent at Campamento, a Spanish village nearby, and we thus grew up bilingual, speaking Spanish nearly as fluently as our native tongue.

In the midst of their happiness came their father Edmund's accident. He used to ride from Campamento to Gibraltar on his English bay mare, Kate, which had been bred for him by the Ingarsby Carvers. A younger son, Richard, always called Ricardo, used to accompany him on his donkey. (Ricardo died at school at Sherborne a few years later.) One day Edmund was giving bread to the donkey before they started. The donkey caught Edmund's finger in his mouth and chewed it. The doctor was sent for. The damaged finger should have been amputated at once, but this was not done until too late and Edmund's arm was badly infected. He returned to England and was attended by leading surgeons but his arm had to be amputated above the elbow and his health was permanently affected. He bore this all with the greatest fortitude and good humour, nursed by his wife Mary and daughter Maggie. After the loss of his arm Mary accompanied him for many years on his travels round the Mediterranean and his daughter Maggie helped run his affairs at the Post Office. He died in 1877 aged sixty-four.

After 'one-armed' Edmund died, his daughter Annie wrote:

My father's friends at the GPO in London, when they heard of his death, cabled out 'Apply for the post for one of the family.' We, out there, presumed this meant one of our brothers should apply for it; but when letters followed the cable it said the application was to be made for my sister Margaret Susan [Maggie, born 1847]. Lord John Manners was Postmaster-General and greatly in favour of gentlewomen being given independent appointments – even though in those days it was quite unheard of. Lord Napier, who was the Governor of Gibraltar, backed up the application, and my sister Margaret Susan was given the appointment of Post Mistress, but not the Surveyorship of the British Post Offices in the Mediterranean. She carried out the work splendidly, backed up by the GPO. She was Head of the British Post Office in Morocco, where she used to ride from place to place on camelback. She retired after thirty years' work and was given the Imperial Service Order.

In later years the family heard a stamp was to be issued in her honour, but nothing came of it.

2

Clans and Quakers

All families, I suppose, have a feeling about who and what they are. My father's family felt themselves to be upper middle class service and professional people. They lived by a code of honour, duty and hard work, and had cast-iron principles of integrity. I don't think many were wealthy, but most seem to have led comfortable lives in the upper ranks of the professions. They were given to a dry humour, with puns in Latin and Greek. They were pretty impressive.

My father was Kenneth Grant Mitchell, called Grant after his great-great-uncle, the Charles Grant whose letter to William Fraser I have already cited. Charles was the son of Alexander Grant, 'The Swordsman', who had long fair hair, and who, with two strokes of the claymore, had slain a mounted Hanoverian trooper who pursued him across the Ness after the Battle of Culloden in 1745. On the eve of the battle thirty clansmen had gathered round Charles's cradle and sworn fealty with clashing swords to Prince Charles Edward, after whom the infant had been named.

The infant Charles grew in poverty to manhood (his father had died of fever at the siege of Havana in 1762). In 1767, at twenty-two, with only a guinea in his pocket, he walked from Dunedin to London where he joined the East India Company. He rose to become Director for twenty-two years. He represented Inverness in Parliament from 1802 to 1818.

I have original letters from Charles Grant to various family members saying that if they would support him as MP for Inverness he would give them unlimited patronage in the East India Company. Charles Grant was, with Wilberforce, a leading member of the 'Clapham Sect' who played a prominent part in the abolition of the slave trade. Wilberforce said of Charles Grant: 'He was the best man I ever knew.'

There was an article by an Indian writer, Vishal Mangalwadi, in the *Daily Mail* of 24 July 1997, entitled 'The Debt My Country Still Owes Britain'. It particularly endorses the good that Charles Grant did for the people of India:

> It is commonplace for the British nowadays to feel guilt over the Indian Empire. Was it not exploitation of the worst kind? The historian Lord Macaulay said at the very beginning of British rule that the East India Company was 'a gang of evil robbers' and their rule in Bengal was 'a government of evil genius'.
>
> But as an Indian, and an author of histories of India, I believe that the British rule in India was a blessing... The beginnings were indeed, as Macaulay said, evil – little more than plunder. But as early as 1793 a junior employee of the East India Company, Charles Grant by name, began to establish a new principle.
>
> It was God who had given India to the British. He would not have done so just so that it could be exploited. He must have had a higher purpose – and that purpose must have been to do good to the Indian people.
>
> Within a few years, Grant was Director of the East India Company – and that principle of government was to last, enshrined by dozens of Acts of Parliament, until the twentieth century. India was to be governed every bit as well as the British governed themselves. That meant the best administration, and with the best of civil servants.

In tracing my Fraser descent I knew that Mary Fraser descended from the Lovat Frasers in the sixteenth century. The Frasers were originally descended from French adventurers – Frizels – who came over from France with the Normans and by degrees moved northwards – from East Lothian and Tweeddale to Invernessshire. Our branch were the Frasers of Farraline and of Balnain.

My contemporary, James Fraser, had had to sell Farraline, a lovely place on the south shores of Loch Ness, and then lived at Tomich, on the edge of Glen Affric. He said he was happy to include me in the Fraser family and that I would be permitted to wear the Fraser sash at any Highland Ball. Not that I had ever been to a Highland Ball, but this new identity prompted me to learn to dance reels with friends in Kent.

The Chief Highland Ball was the Northern Meeting. It was instigated in 1788. To heal the diverse wounds after the defeat at Culloden of Bonnie Prince Charlie, whose rebellion had divided Scotland, thirteen gentlemen of the Highlands (including two of my Fraser forebears), met to promote social intercourse: 'games for the people and balls for the gentry'. Hence the Northern Meeting, a gathering of the clans in and around Inverness where 'social intercourse' was promoted by dancing traditional Highland reels far into the night. I went to it, wearing my Fraser sash, for nearly twenty years.

We also descend from Dr Thomas Fraser of Antigua. He married Elizabeth Mackinnon, one of the 'Mackinnon children' in the portrait by Hogarth that now hangs in the National Gallery of Ireland in Dublin. Her brother William, the other child in the portrait, bought Acrise Place in Kent, some ten miles away from Godmersham Park where Jane Austen wrote *Mansfield Park*. I had a flight of fancy over this connection. In *Mansfield Park* Jane Austen states that the Bertram family got into mischief while the head of the family was 'absent on business in Antigua'. The Mackinnon connection seems very possible.

We have already touched on the Creswells. My father's cousin Gordon Creswell, seriously wounded by a leopard in South Africa, had his vessel sunk under him three times when taking part in the D-Day landings in the Second World War. Another cousin, Hector, Rear-Admiral Creswell, CB, was Cutlass Champion of the Navy and became Commodore of convoys to Britain from New York and Murmansk. My Great-Uncle Willy, Vice-Admiral Sir William

Creswell, started the Australian Navy and became its first Commander-in-Chief. He served successfully against Arab slave traders and received thanks from Lord Salisbury, the British Foreign Minister of the day. The naval Creswells were successful almost everywhere – there was a family saying: 'The sun never sets on the British Empire, nor on the Creswell family, as there is one in every naval station around the world.'

Another cousin, Michael Creswell, passed second into the Diplomatic Service. He was First Secretary in Madrid during the war, and advised the family that they were not going to be allowed to keep their houses in Campamento under wartime Spanish legislation. So he, Michael, thought it best to take them over. He did so and then set up his wife Elizabeth in one of them before departing for his next posting to Teheran. There he met the wife of the Dutch Ambassador to Persia. She said to me, many years later, 'How could I help loving him?' She was Mea, Baroness Theo Schwartzenburg en Hohenlansberg. He later married her and left Elizabeth forlorn in the house at Campamento. Elizabeth later told me that she still loved him and was heartbroken. Michael and Mea had a son called Alexander – a contemporary of our sons at Winchester – who became a noted watercolour artist with royal commissions to paint Windsor Castle after the fire and again after the restoration – the pictures were shown in a gallery in Windsor Castle – and more recently to paint the Queen Mother's lying-in-state in Westminster Hall, as a personal request from the Queen.

Michael became Ambassador to the Argentine, Yugoslavia and Finland. He never achieved any of the most coveted diplomatic positions but he is remembered as a member of the Secret Service trio named 'Saturday', 'Sunday' and 'Monday'. The first of these was Airey Neave, whose book *Saturday at MI9* recorded his exploits in the agency which specialised in helping Allied servicemen escape from Occupied Europe. 'Sunday', Donald Darling, operated in Lisbon under the cover of a vice consul in charge of refugees. Michael, from the cover of the Madrid embassy, formed a third and vital link as 'Monday' in what became known as the Comet Line, spiriting aircrew back to Britain. He worked closely with Andrée (Dedée) de Jongh, the Belgian woman who was awarded the George Medal for her work in the line, and she flew from Brussels to attend Michael's funeral in Surrey. My old friend Bob (Air Marshal Sir Lewis) Hodges, the head of the 'Escapers Club', introduced us. The gallant little Contesse de Jongh used to cross Occupied France with escapers and take them to a rendezvous in the Pyrenees where she met Michael. He took them on down to Campamento and settled them in his safe houses there until they could be sailed out across the bay of Algeciras to waiting British destroyers. Any wounded were cared for by the barber at the Rock Hotel. Catita Lumley, the wife of Christie's representative in Kent, was brought out by the Comet Line with her parents.

My mother's family, the Westlakes, were Quakers, a religious sect, originally the Society of Friends, founded by George Fox in 1650. Their views were to the right of the Puritans, of whom there were many in America. George Fox said that his people 'trembled at the word of God', but the name Quaker was more likely due to their trembling and shaking at their religious meetings. They were against all frills in speech, dress, and manners, strongly against the use of alcohol, and did not support Oxford or Cambridge universities.

Quakers had very strong views on how their followers should behave, as the following little tale shows. Here is corrective morality in full flower.

The year was 1838. Caroline Capper was sitting trying to stitch and thinking of a young man who had paid her a visit last week and whom she hoped to see again.

Then there came a knock upon the door, and in he came.

'I am so pleased to find thee alone, Miss Capper.'
'I welcome thee, sir. My mamma will very shortly return.'
'May I then rapidly explain myself to thee? I am Edward

Westlake, who came to this city from the nearby countryside, and earlier from Devon, in order to make my fortune. My business has prospered but of friends I had found none and was lonely in this busy town. Until the folk where I lodge advised me to join the Society of Friends which some call Quakers.

'It was at the meeting House of the Friends that I first saw thee, so modest in deportment, so plainly attired, so excellent in behaviour and so beautiful, that I wished to learn more about thee and hoped that thou might become my real friend. It is wonderful to me that the Quakers have no worldly ideas, are always truthful, and aim to be goodness itself which indeed thou appearest to be. This is such a happy change from some city dwellers whose apparel is so bright and flashy who wear much shining jewellery and behave in a loud fashion, so that I wish to understand thee who are so unworldly and so good. Please advise me.'

'Well, sir, there is little to tell thee. I do indeed try to live as the Society of Friends would wish and would be happy to be thy friend. But I do have worldly thoughts on which I try not to dwell. Even last week my papa told me and my sisters that he would take us to the theatre that very afternoon. This was a pleasure that we had never dreamed would be permitted to us.

'We assembled in the hall decently attired in gloves, bonnets and pelisses. Then my papa came in and said, "Thou art not going to the theatre today, nor any day. I told thee to make certain that thou canst all brook disappointment in a comely manner. So take off thy pelisses, thy gloves and bonnets, and go to thy rooms with a smile on thy faces to show thou art able to brook disappointment by thy good behaviour."

'We all smiled at our papa and took off our bonnets. I went to my bedchamber and I wept for half an hour. So my behaviour was very worldly for which I should be ashamed. Also as I am not permitted to tell a lie I now must tell thee that when thou camest to visit me last time thy question led me into a sore problem that I cannot overcome. Thou asked me "What art thou sewing, Miss Capper?"

'Because I was so embarrassed to tell the truth I said "I am making curtains for the dining room." I must now tell the truth, I was in fact making lady's drawers. My mamma, who was present and said I should never tell a lie, ordered me to unpick the drawers and to turn them into dining room curtains. I have tried and tried but I have found this to be an impossible task all because I told a lie to thee. Perhaps thou canst understand and find it in thy heart to forgive me, sir.'

'Not only do I understand but I honour thee for thy modest behaviour and of course I forgive thee. Perhaps now thou couldst help me. Please Miss Capper, because next week is my birthday and I would wish for a friend with whom to celebrate, wouldst thou as my friend attend the theatre in my company and afterwards sup with me at a local hostelry where I hope to present thee with some modest jewellery – a small ring as a token of my appreciation, and I hope I may also say of my affection for thee.'

'Dear sir, thou knowest that I cannot tell a lie. It would give me the greatest pleasure to celebrate thy birthday in thy company as I anticipate with extreme delight my enjoyment of a worldly evening as thy friend.'

Edward Westlake and Caroline Capper were married in 1839. This marriage produced thirteen children, of whom my grandfather Edward was the eldest son. The Westlakes lived for several generations in a handsome stone house called Silvermere, overlooking the River Itchen, and were wheat importers and also traders in sacks (for wheat I suppose). In the 1920s on every Southern Railway station there used to be the well-known enamel sign of an ink splash for Stephens ink, and alongside a sign for Westlakes' sacks. My grandfather as the eldest son must have inherited the family business interests in and around Southampton, to which he proved to be ill-suited.

Several of his sisters married: Juliet married Charles Garton, brewer and owner of many public houses. Juliet must have been the leader in family prayers, maybe due to her conscience being greatly troubled because her husband was making a huge fortune out of drink. She held family prayers every weekday morning at the long breakfast table. Those of the family staying in the house sat in a row behind her, the housekeeper in a place superior to the other servants, who filed in in strict order of precedence. The butler, the cook, the parlourmaid, the senior housemaid, and others, down to the most recently employed kitchenmaid. Up to about fifteen people.

The morning prayers of Juliet's daughter Lois, who married Bishop Rose in Canterbury, were similar. Any visiting tradesmen – say the carpenter, the fishmonger, or even the postman – who happened to arrive at the time, were brought into the dining room and on to their knees as well.

Edward's sister Ellen married the Revd Albert Hudson, vicar of Bingley, with whom I stayed as a girl. Her breakfast prayers were impressive. All the staff attended and knelt against the chairs around the wall – backs to the breakfast table. I remember finding the array of blue uniformed bottoms with white starched belts and cuffs an impressive sight, something one could never see today.

The Hudsons were a very gifted family, who followed the developing artistic interests of the day. They lived at Bushey Heath in a handsome house, and had a large kiln in the garden where they had produced fine handmade pots. The eldest son Cyril became a well-known eye surgeon. He had a fabulous collection of small *objets d'art*, and lived in Queen Anne Street, ruled by his aged staff. On one particular day I lunched with him on delicious cold salmon.

'Could I please have a slice of bread, Uncle Cyril, to eat with my salmon?'

The reply was 'Do you think you could do without?' He did not wish to ask his aged servants to climb up from the basement where they worked. I did without.

His brother Wilfred lived a dilettante existence, as he had no need to earn a living. He took to watercolour painting in his forties, and was showing in the famous Paris Salon a couple of years later. My early interest in painting was aroused by sitting beside asthmatic old Wilfrid, wheezing away while little masterpieces flowed off his brush.

His sister Hilda was a brilliant portrait painter and showed at the Royal Academy. She was more than slightly potty and would invite all and sundry to sit for her. As a result, her basement became home for a collection of 'down and outs' with interesting faces, who decided to take up residence. The local vicar begged her family to make a concerted effort to rid her of these undesirables.

When he was a young man, my grandfather, Edward Westlake, visited the then fashionable Blackheath, where he met and married the beautiful Maud Godsal. She was partly French and very attractive. She wore pretty, soft colours, quite unlike the usual Quaker dress that I remember, of floor-length brown silk dresses, buttoned up to the neck with long sleeves. My grandfather was very artistic and good at drawing. He was also very musical. He bought one of the first pianolas (a mechanical piano player), on which he played endless rolls of Lizst, his favourite composer. My mother, Lilian Westlake, was so pretty, clever and lively that I feel she must have taken after some of her French ancestors, rather than after the sedate Quakers.

3
The Mitchells

My grandfather Hugh Mitchell was the only son of Hugh and Jessie Mitchell. In 1875, at the age of twenty-six, he was posted to Gibraltar. He had won a scholarship from Cheam to Harrow, and was at Randalls House, Harrow, from 1864 to 1867. He won a number of prizes for classics and mathematics and was captain of shooting. He was commissioned into the Royal Engineers in 1869, giving him possibly more scope than joining the Indian Army as his father had done. After Woolwich, where he was for a time a contemporary of Kate Creswell's brother Edmund, he was posted to Bermuda, then Gibraltar. His father, Colonel Hugh, had served in the East India Company's Madras Light Infantry and had retired originally to Nice, but died in London when his son Hugh was only eleven years old.

Kate Creswell was seventeen when Hugh was posted to Gibraltar. There must have been a very active social life in Gibraltar in the 1870s, as it was one of the main staging posts of Empire. It was run by the Governor and his administration (which included Kate's sister Maggie). It had a sizeable military garrison and was frequently the port of call for naval vessels whose officers would come ashore to find recuperation and entertainment. It was also a trading centre. The Carvers had developed a major cotton exporting business through Gibraltar – they later brought Egyptian cotton imports from Alexandria. The Creswells, mainly the Lisbon branch, were not only wine exporters but cork exporters as well. They too had a large business, with their own cork forests in Portugal.

Hugh Mitchell left for England at the end of his posting in 1878 and so did Kate, and they were married that year at White Notley in Essex by her mother's Fraser half-brother. Hugh was posted to the Staff College and later to the Intelligence Department in the

War Office in 1881. Their children were born in rapid succession, Katharine in 1879, Hugh in 1880, Alan in 1882. How to educate his growing family on a soldier's pay must have been foremost in Hugh's mind when he started reading for the Bar in 1881. He was called to the Bar in 1884 – to the Inner Temple. Briefs were slow in coming to a newly qualified barrister, so at a friend's instigation, and to add to their income, the couple set up a business as crammers for Army entrants. They moved to a larger house in 6 Douro Place, Kensington to accommodate their family and Army pupils.

Kate died aged thirty-five in 1892, a few days after giving birth to their youngest boy, Amyot. Hugh Mitchell got a cable from Kate's sister Maggie (later renowned as Post Mistress of the Mediterranean) to say there was an opening for a barrister in Gibraltar and nearby Morocco, and she welcomed him and all his family to stay. So my grandfather removed himself and his seven motherless children to Gibraltar to stay with his sister-in-law Maggie, to practise as a barrister there, and in Morocco. It was said he might have been more successful had the Spaniards not preferred their barristers more devious.

Hugh Mitchell lived in Campamento for thirty years, during which time he rented three different houses. Stables were an important part of all of them as he used to ride daily to his office in Gibraltar across the sands of the Bay. Also the boys loved their ponies (they were believed on one occasion to hunt two to a pony). I have a picture of my father at about twelve years old, hunting on a donkey with the Calpe Hunt. They lived near the sea where they kept a sailing boat, so that they had their diversions. Katharine, his eldest child and only daughter, he kept at home, educating her himself. I was told she wanted to get married to a suitable young man, but was prevented by her father – enough to sour her for life, but in spite of this she looked after him for over fifty years.

The loss of Kate was a lasting grief. Robbed of her 'loving prevailing presence' he appears to have withdrawn into intellectual pursuits, which distanced him from his children. He taught the boys at home to prepare them for their boarding schools. He encouraged all his family to study the classics and the table conversation tended to be laced with Latin quips or Greek puns. He daily read the morning newspapers in five languages – important doubtless for his legal business, but a demanding task for most people. I now realise how greatly his children must have suffered too from their mother's loss, Katharine in particular.

The eldest son was Hugh. No Mitchells were soft and he certainly wasn't. He was a mining engineer (his father being a Sapper may have been an influence in his choice of career) and he worked in South Africa, manager of the biggest of the Rand gold mining companies. I was invited to go down his gold mine when I was about seventeen. He showed me a gold brick. 'You can have it if you can lift it,' he said. Of course there wasn't a hope, and there it stayed. He never married and was certainly not comfortable with the ladies. When I was a girl I went with him and Aunt Kay to the Johannesburg Exhibition in 1936. He marched in front with his hands behind his back and seemed quite unaware that we were present. A little consideration of females would have been nice. He had a large house and beautiful garden in Johannesburg and at a family gathering there a uniformed servant came out to our party under the trees with a tray of tinkling glasses, and someone remarked 'There's something to be said for "roughing it" in the Colonies.' Hugh ran a fine farm and bred pointer dogs in Natal.

The next son, Alan MacCaskill, I think profited from his father's coaching. He won a scholarship to Peterhouse, Cambridge, where he read classics, and passed well into the Indian Civil Service. He served in the Punjab and his daughter remembers as a child riding on yaks over the border into Tibet, with a spare yak with milk for the baby. Alan got typhoid as a young man and died of it on the eve of his retirement when he would have been due for a knighthood, after a distinguished career in India.

My father, Kenneth Grant, I think suffered the most. He was seven when his mother died and while the others were either at school or in Gibraltar, he had to stay alone with his father being coached for entry into Colet Court. I believe it was a daunting and solitary experience.

Edmund became a mining engineer and joined his brother in South Africa who looked after him. He lost his left arm in the war. He was a sad case. All the family loved Edmund, who had great charm and friendliness. Shelagh Stuttaford, of the large South African store business, said that he had been a wonderful stepfather to her. His drink problem, we learned at the end of his life, was made to seem far worse due to his having had undiagnosed arterial sclerosis for a long time.

Philip could well have done with a motherly eye on him to save him getting up to tricks. His father used to summon Philip to sit in front of him in order to admire Philip's Greek profile. Not really helpful to Philip I suspect, but he did win a classical scholarship to Trinity, Oxford. Here he was very idle and got into what used to be called 'fast company', whose larks included once painting the noses of the statues red. His scholarship was taken away and his father said he could not keep him at Oxford without one. So he had to leave. His subsequent experiences were written by himself – *Forty Years Back*:

There was, of course, no 'Colonial Service' to join in 1912. Each country had its own, recruited in various ways. First there were the 'failed I.C.S.' countries. You entered for the Indian Civil Service examination, as it was called. If you passed in the first ten or twelve you normally went to the Home Service, wore a black felt hat and worked from 11 a.m. to 6 p.m. daily with a generous gap in the middle for lunch at your club. The next forty or so were appointed to the Indian Civil Service. Then came what were called Eastern Cadetships, that is administrative appointments to Hong Kong, the Federated Malay States and Ceylon, under the Colonial Office; so incredibly idle had I been at Oxford that I failed even to find a place among the Eastern Cadets.

The second way into the Colonial Service then was to have

a relative who was a Governor and took you out as private secretary, as often as not unpaid; once in his satrapy, there was no serious difficulty in obtaining a permanent appointment.

Finally, there was a simple process of applying for a post in some Colony. There was a Patronage Committee to select applicants and the Private Secretary to the Secretary of State ran the business; it seems hardly credible, but it is true, that in 1912 that post was occupied by Mortimer Durand, a distinguished cousin of my father's who had begun his career in the Indian Civil Service and ended it as Ambassador to Washington. Peculiar as it may sound today, he was chairman of the admirably named Patronage Committee. This seemed to me, rightly as the event proved, to be likely to result in the committee feeling a robust confidence in my suitability for colonial administration. A cynical uncle told me about this time that I could not hope for a post in a habitable country, because these all went to the Little Brothers of the Rich, and I certainly was not that. But, he added cheerfully, there was always the White Man's grave for which the Little Brothers were not applicants and Cousin Mortimer would no doubt see that I got a post there – that is to say in West Africa or the unhealthy parts of the East.

So it proved; if memory is not playing tricks I had the choice of the Sudan at £400 a year, or Nyasaland at £250. Probably the Sudan post was for the contract districts in the south, for the central and northern Sudan was jealously guarded Little Brother country. It is in any case incredible that I should have refused £400 a year in a country of unlimited £10 ponies in favour of £250 in Nyasaland, even though I did not know until I got there that there were no ponies at all.

The next thing after being appointed was to attend a course at the Imperial Institute, which lasted ten weeks and in which lectures were given on criminal law by an agreeably convivial Irish barrister; on accounts by the then Director of Colonial Audit – who told us that the Colonial system of accounting was the most beautiful thing he had encountered in his life (what a life!); on tropical hygiene, and on surveying. The surveying consisted of walking about Banstead Downs humping strange instruments and calling frequently at the local pubs for beer. We liked our instructor greatly, I remember, and viewed the mysteries in which he tried to instruct us without alarm, because we soon came to learn that, when the time came for the examination, his clerk was in the habit of supplying the 'students' with all the material necessary to answer the paper correctly, for a modest fee.

The tropical hygiene lecturer was a gloomy leech who had been for a short time in Nyasaland, had contracted blackwater fever and returned to England. He took each tropical disease in turn, described its symptoms and so on and ended 'And the result is death'. One day, I suppose meaning to cheer us up, he varied this formula by saying: 'But I do not want you to suppose that the result is in every case immediately fatal; sometimes the patient lingers on for a few days', then, after a pause for reflection, 'in frightful agony'. It seemed that Nyasaland was the White Man's grave all right!

On some days there would be three lectures, on others two, occasionally only one; so I went round to the Colonial Office and asked if there was any other form of instruction with which I might usefully fill in the ample spare time. A bright young man told me that if I was going to Nyasaland he advised me to learn to shoe a horse, 'for', he said, 'there is not a farrier in the Protectorate'. So I arranged to learn, for a modest fee and certainly with toil, sweat and some blood, if not tears, on the vast feet of dray and 'bus horses at the forge which then existed near the Common end of Wimbledon High Street. I was brought up on horseback, but one of the things I had not learned was shoeing. It was then that I acquired that awe-struck respect for the vast knowledge of the Colonial Office that I have retained ever since. For that young man was perfectly right; there was not a farrier in Nyasaland. True, there was not a horse either, but that was no doubt the business of another department.

Well, at last all the preliminaries were over, even including the purchase of an incredible amount of quite useless junk. Every young man going out to Africa bought, for instance, a portable berkefeld filter, an object called a Lord's lamp, another kind of lamp with no chimney and a clockwork-driven fan in the base, a fitted cook's box with a vast assortment of pots and pans, each neatly in its own compartment of Venesta wood – a challenge which no African cook could resist, of course. The partitions were soon broken or discarded and the gear reduced to frying pan, kettle and saucepan, and perhaps a knife that was more often worn at the cook's belt, like a dagger. We bought, too, vast pith helmets, spine pads, cholera belts and the Lord alone knows how much other junk. You could buy it all, new and unused, with the names of your predecessors stencilled on it, especially filters and lamps, for a few shillings at any of the junk sales that were such a feature of life in remote places in those days. But nobody told you that in London, and the admirable colonial outfitting firms who competed for our custom and cheerfully gave us long credit had a very persuasive way with them and sold these peculiarly useless and cumbersome things to us in great quantities. You could buy anything a man really needed, at half the prices paid in London, in the general stores of any African Colony – but, again, nobody told us that in London; and if we had been told we should not have believed it. For the truth is, we all felt like a lot of young Stanleys and Spekes and the more exotic and peculiar the things we bought, the more we felt like intrepid explorers bound on some romantic 'Mission to the Interior'.

Junk and all I duly embarked on the German East Africa Line's *Feldmarschal*, and after a leisurely journey that included the Suez Canal, Aden, Mombasa, Tanga, Zanzibar and Dar-es-Salaam, arrived off the Chinde mouth of the

Zambesi, and by stern-wheel steamer and little wood-burning train at Limbe in the Shire Highlands.

Those were the great days of the big-game hunters. Wealthy men and even a few women – and there were many rich then – mostly from the United Kingdom, but a few Americans, Frenchmen and others, betook themselves via Mombasa and Nairobi to the vast game plains of Kenya, so that the Kedong Valley, the Lorian Swamp, Laikipia and other remote places were as full of dukes, marquesses and what have you as the Royal Enclosure at Ascot. And, if we impecunious cadets bought a lot of junk, these mighty hunters brought wagon loads of it, most of which they doubtless gave to their White Hunters unused – for even by then we could not be just hunters, we had to be white! The extraordinary obsessions with 'heads' and other trophies and records of big game was all the rage. Admirable men, the soul of honour in other things, would squeeze and twist their little steel tapes to try and make the horn of some unsightly mammal an eighth of an inch longer; would lie like lawyers to their cronies about the vast spread of buffalo horns or the weight of tusks, and would lie awake at night dreaming of the day when they might see in Rowland Ward's *Records of Big Game*, 'Hartebeest, John Smith, Nyasaland, 12⅜ inches.'

I suppose there was some sense in it for the owners of ancestral halls, at any rate in the case of the more imposing and decorative heads, such as the kudu, the oryx or the buffalo; but what an impecunious Administrative Cadet supposed he was going to do with the smelly remains of heads that he so zealously collected, I cannot now imagine. And yet, when I first went on leave nine years later – seven years over-due because of the Kaiser's War – my baggage smelt to high heaven, for it consisted largely of skins and heads for the curing and mounting of which I paid large sums I could ill afford. Where they all went to in the end, I have long since forgotten.

Arrived in Zomba, I reported to the Secretariat, my first experience of that remarkable institution. I remember that I was told that I had been posted to Mzimba, some hundreds of miles away in the north. When I asked how I got there I got the, to me then, surprising answer, 'Walk.' Being strongly of the same mind as Cobbett (of *Rural Rides*), who wrote 'Doubtless had God meant man to walk he would have given him four legs, like the beasts', I took a poor view of this. But, as I have just said, it was my first experience of Secretariats; I need not have worried. In the next two or three weeks I was posted to Fort Johnston, to Liwonde, to Blantyre and to Zomba itself; in the end I found myself at Mlanje and was left there for fifteen whole months. I suppose the posting game was being played with someone else by then.

And when, being young, foolish and bursting with zeal to start this Sanders of the River business, I intruded upon my first boss as soon as he came to the office one morning and nervously asked if he could tell me what my duties were, he raised a pale, anaemic countenance, looked at me for a bit with pain and marked distaste and then replied: 'Yes, I can; to keep out of my sight.'

Philip's mother had died when he was only two, so he had never known a happy family life. If he had done so he could never have said he would 'marry the first woman to beat him at golf' – which he did. He had otherwise a brilliant career. He won the MC in the war, became Governor of Uganda, then Wavell's Chief Political Officer and a major-general. He organised the administration of East Africa after the defeat of the Italians in Ethiopia and had successful negotiations with the Emperor Haile Selassie. With the entry of Japan into the war he was sent to govern Fiji to exert his influence in that theatre. He returned to become Governor of Kenya and was generally considered the finest African administrator since Lord Lugard and due for a peerage. Fate was not so kind and my husband Bill's note explains:

[31]

I was head of the Middle East Security Intelligence organisation (SIME) from 1945 to 1951. My area consisted of Greece and Turkey in Southern Europe; the whole Middle East from the eastern frontier of Libya to and including Persia; East Africa including the Sudan and Ethiopia to the northern frontier of Rhodesia. It therefore included Kenya.

The colonies and other territories in the area were responsible for their own internal security from espionage, subversion and sabotage and for having an internal security organisation for that purpose. It was my responsibility to visit and to advise them on their security organisation and to pass them any relevant external information that I might receive.

When I visited Kenya I knew that the colony had no internal security organisation. Sir Philip Mitchell, Maxine's uncle, was the Governor and I strongly advised him to set up an internal security organisation. He said there was no need. The police special branch, the missionaries, British resident farmers and businessmen would know all that was going on, and would inform him.

I told him that Moscow was determined to subvert the British Empire and was sending trained people into the colonies to organise under-cover subversive organisations which would strike at the administration when the time was ripe. These organisations would be such as to evade normal police investigation and would only be discovered by trained security service type people. I undertook to train his people if he would set up such an organisation.

He would have none of it. He said he was quite satisfied with his existing intelligence cover, and preferred to spend the limited money he had on education, to which cause he was particularly devoted.

Eventually his time as Governor of Kenya came to an end. He had also reached the age of retirement. He was an exceptionally able man and much the most distinguished official in the colonial service and it became generally known that he would receive a peerage.

But soon after his retirement, very serious trouble broke out in Kenya, conducted by a subversive organisation known as the Mau-Mau. Mau-Mau cells were active all over the country and it took a major police and military effort to suppress them.

Mitchell, just retired, was blamed for not having been aware of the existence of the Mau-Mau and its threat to peace in Kenya. His reputation was severely damaged and he did not receive his peerage.

He was too good a man to suffer such a fate, and perhaps I am partly to blame for failing to persuade him to be adequately covered in security matters.

Uncle Phil had very little money to spend. He considered it of vital importance to spend it on education of the Africans and he had been instrumental in establishing Makerere University. He was probably right in the long term but not in the short term. Bill was certainly not to blame. Uncle Phil's plan for the education of Africans has proved to be most successful. We are familiar now with Africans as academics, politicians and diplomats. At the same time it must be said that Moscow had completely undermined the power of the British Empire.

I thought my Uncle Phil a lovely man. He was very kind and good to me when I stayed with him in Uganda when my mother was ill. He stopped at Gibraltar on his way home to England after retirement on his farm in Kenya and was delighted to talk Spanish again. He became ill and finally died in Gibraltar. He was buried with full military honours at the foot of the Rock. A fitting finale to the family's connection there.

4
Childhood Years

My father was an engineer who had decided to go to India to make his life designing and building roads and bridges. His first job was working on the first dry dock in Southampton, and in his spare time he enjoyed playing rugger against the local team. The captain of the team was Max Westlake, my mother's brother. She used to love watching their games, and it was here she met my father, and eventually they got engaged. They decided that he should go to India as planned, and when he was established in his career, she would follow him to India to get married, which she did, with her Quaker cousin Bee Lewis, in 1912. Bee Lewis travelled with a hatbox at least a metre square, carrying the large hat she proposed to wear at their wedding in Bombay.

Their journey to Bombay will have been by steamship through the Suez Canal and the Red Sea. On this journey it was preferable to be POSH, and have your stateroom Port Out, Starboard Home, which meant you were on the right side of the steamship to escape the heat. It was less costly to travel in a cabin on the deck below, where portholes were fitted with large windscoops to draw whatever breezes there may have been in the Red Sea into the sultry cabins. This must have been the way Lilian and her cousin Bee Lewis travelled in 1912.

The early days of a young engineer and his wife in India were rugged, exciting, and dangerous. My father was posted to the Punjab and to the North West Frontier where good communications were badly needed. He had to prospect for possible roads along rocky precipices, above racing torrents, over sandy deserts, and in deep jungle. My mother used to accompany him, usually on camelback, sometimes on elephants, to camp sites set up as they travelled through the wildest parts, often through unfriendly tribal territory. They carried all their tent equipment, bedding, food and gear on the backs of camel or mule transport, and travelled with their staff and servants, who were also loaded with their own equipment, in a cavalcade of at least twenty people. They had to cross streams and rivers on rafts of inflated buffalo skins.

Later, when they had one of the first touring cars, this had to be driven on to a much larger raft and poled across the immense width of rivers swollen by the rain. Eventually my father created his soaring bridges built to stand up to the pressure of these rivers, and made the first tarmac roads that could not be washed away in the seasonal floods. My mother always had her spaniels with her and I think found her early adventures exhilarating.

They were then posted to Rawalpindi on the North West Frontier, where I was born in 1916. My mother had hoped to have a son, to be called Max after her brother, and I was a disappointment, so she called me Maxine. Three of my mother's friends had babies at the same time and all were brought up together by our Indian ayahs, who cared for us devotedly. My father was then promoted and moved to Lahore, the capital of the Punjab.

My mother, always travelling with my father around India, had never had a home for more than six months in any place and perhaps her dream of settling down in an old stone house near an English village with a walled garden and a cedar tree was passed on to me. She never achieved her dream. Most of her adult life had been spent in India, with an annual move from the Lahore plains to Simla in the Himalayan foothills and back again. Twice a year the grand piano was shifted up 6,000 feet by truck, rail, and mountain railway and then on the backs of about six men to the beautiful single storey house on the hillside. Here it was installed in the pretty white painted drawing room, where my father would sing his repertoire of after-dinner drawing room ballads. 'Pale hands I loved beside the Shalimar' would alternate with 'Sweet Little Buttercup' and the whole gamut of Gilbert and Sullivan.

My parents would ride out in the evening to watch the famous amateur theatricals in the Simla 'Green Room' and there was little other form of public entertainment. My father told me that on one occasion his evening trousers had got such a soaking on his ride that he had to remove them, wring them out and hang them up to dry in the back of the box while the theatrical performance was in progress.

I so much enjoyed my life as a child with my attractive, vivacious mother, to whom all her household was devoted. I don't think my father, who had lost his own mother when very young, was ever happy until he met and married my mother. Although she came of a Quaker family she was most unlike one's idea of a 'Quaker girl'. Vivacious and pretty, she was a very good bridge player, and an excellent tennis player. She had a spinning underhand serve (no one served overhand in those days) and was much in demand as a player for her clever control of the ball.

My first memory of her is when she came home from tennis calling, 'The war is ended. The war is ended.' Another early memory was more traumatic. My great treat was to have tea with her in the drawing room where she told me stories and would read to me. We sat close together on the sofa behind her silver teapot and silver hot water jug. On one occasion she was wearing a fashionable 'tea gown', of pink chiffon velvet with long hanging cuffs. One of these caught in the hot water jug. I remember the pain of scalding water cascading over my bare legs. My mother was shocked and distressed, calling for a peon to go for the doctor. The burns took weeks to heal. I never for a moment felt any reproach for my mother.

In Lahore, in the Punjab, we had many Indian servants, due to their caste system. All of them tried to spoil me, pressing me to try jelabies, sticky fried Indian sweets. In our early years we were educated by governesses, our lessons usually shared by other children. I remember classes in the heat of Lahore, the sun shining in striped patterns through 'chicks' – blinds made of bamboo strips – along the verandas, where our wicker chairs creaked in the heat and the punkahs stirred the pages of our copybooks on the desks. During breaks we would play games among the flamboyant scarlet and gold canna lilies, their huge flowers blooming high above our heads. Or we would make forbidden mud pies which set like cement in the heat and which were lovingly decorated with cosmos and strong-smelling marigolds.

In the evenings our Italian governess and our ayah, our loving Indian nurse, used to take us for sedate walks through the Lawrence gardens in the centre of Lahore. Here bats roosted like fruit high up in the eucalyptus trees, bright green parrots flashed through the undergrowth and the peacocks in the gardens used to scream at each other. More worrying were the bats, clouds of them, reputed to get tangled in one's hair. I was always anxious to leave the gardens before they appeared and flew squeaking off into the gathering dusk.

Occasionally we visited the Shalimar Gardens outside the city walls. Those famous gardens had been laid out in 1641 by the Mogul Emperor Shah Jehan, who had also built the Taj Mahal as a memorial to his beloved wife, Mumtaz. Shalimar Gardens became world famous – originally they had 3 terraces and 429 fountains, and finally provided a setting for the magnificent sandstone tomb of Shah Jehan himself. The tomb was ornate, and lavishly decorated with beautiful inlaid mosaics representing flowers. Over time, the gardens and buildings fell into decay, but were later restored and cared for by the Archaeological Department of the British Government. Peacocks and peahens were introduced to strut along the ancient terraces and I loved to watch them showing off their brilliant fantails, they were so beautiful. Their screaming voices are another matter.

The Mogul Emperors were originally Mongols descended from Genghis Khan. Their empire covered all of India and the capital was originally Agra, but as the Afghan tribes increasingly threatened their northern borders, the Moguls had to remove their capital from Agra to more northern Lahore, thus beginning the decline and final fall of the Mogul Empire, to be taken over eventually by the British Government.

When the British Government took over the administration of the defunct Mogul empire, the head of the British administration in

Lahore at that time, the Chief Commissioner, was my uncle Alan Mitchell. My father (his brother), Kenneth Grant Mitchell, was also a high-ranking official, responsible for all roads and communications in the Province.

Of course the British officials had their families with them. When it became too hot for families to remain in the heat of the plains in Lahore, they moved up to Simla in the Himalayan foothills. My own family was no exception. We rented a different house most years. One was perched among cascades of pale yellow Banksia roses with breathtaking views of the perpetual Himalayan snows stretched right across our horizon. There was so little room on these precipitous slopes of Simla that only the Viceroy and the Commander-in-Chief had cars. We all rode, walked, or travelled in rickshaws pulled by four coolies. Many of these rickshaw coolies had walked for several days from tiny farms on far distant Himalayan hillsides where their harvest of golden maize used to dry in the sunshine. But with the crops often scanty, the more able-bodied members of these families had to seek additional incomes, which is why they sought work as rickshaw coolies. One of them also used to care for my donkey, and would accompany me on my rides. My donkey regularly used to buck me off on encountering invisible roadside terrors at one particular corner, or just when he wanted to get home faster to his hillside stable. My donkey minder would pick me up and dust off my precious topee – a hard little sunhat wreathed with a muslin frill and, in my view, most exquisite artificial buttercups and daisies. These were my pride and joy and had to be saved from damage, and a dented hat was hard to explain away to a severe Italian governess, who always seemed to be cross.

When the rain came in the monsoon the distant Himalayas became invisible for months on end. The clouds concealed even the top of Jacko, the hill round which Simla was built, and wreathed the hillsides along which I still had to get to my first school. My topee was then covered in a special waterproof covering and my donkey and I slithered along soaking hillside paths through forests of dripping rhododendron and deodar. It was often safer to walk as there was real danger of the hillside slipping away in watery land-slides. Dried watercourses had turned overnight into noisy crash-ing torrents, and their fern-edged gullies needed careful negotiation. But the monsoon rains brought the flowers, and my path to school was not only edged with violets but with abundant lilies of the valley, whose fragrance I can still recall. Flowers have always been one of my greatest pleasures.

When my parents were due to move to an area notoriously unhealthy, if not lethal, for children, I was sent to boarding school in England with my young brother Sprag. He was five and I was eight years old and it was my responsibility to look after him.

This school was an inspired choice of our parents, as it had a wonderful family atmosphere. It was run by a large family, the Hicksons, who had children of their own. One was born while I was there, which I found very exciting. It was the only place in which we were rooted for more than six months at any time. As there were both boys and girls at Oldfeld, we had masters as well as mistresses. This was occasionally alarming to me. When we had mental arithmetic, we all stood up in a row, in front of the head-master beside his blackboard, while he rattled off questions on sums to us. When I gave a wrong answer, I either had to dodge a piece of chalk or board rubber thrown at me, or be sent to the bottom of the class, which was safer, as the headmaster was a good shot. Otherwise, we found the young masters were very soft with the girls, and we could usually wheedle them into helping us with our prep. On the other hand, a black mark for our work could only be expiated by digging up daisies from the cricket pitch. For a misdemeanour, up to a hundred daisies had to be meticulously laid out and counted. I quite enjoyed this task of using my little dibber in the grass.

My mother's life had had to be shared between her husband in India and her children in England. Once every eighteen months she would return to England and take a furnished house for our school holidays and we would enjoy a brief spell of family life. My father could only return every three years, so I only saw him three times while I was at school.

When my father came home he bought an enormous Armstrong-Siddeley open touring car, with a silver-studded bonnet. He used to take us all for wonderful picnics in the New Forest. Other children with parents abroad were not so lucky. The Kaye family had not seen their father for many years, and waited eagerly for his arrival. Imagine everyone's consternation when they greeted the taxi driver in mistake for their father.

Aunt Bee was an elegant, upright maiden lady, the Quaker cousin of my mother, the one had originally acted as my mother's chaperone when she travelled out to India to be married. Aunt Bee later made a holiday home for children of families whose parents were abroad. My brother and I were added to the string of young people whom Aunt Bee tried to rule with a rod of iron. My brother was christened Kenneth Amyot, but my father was reading Surtees's *Mr Sponge's Sporting Tour* when he was born, and said that his new-born son was exactly like Jack Spraggon the boxer. My brother was always called Sprag thereafter.

He was good at all sport and a few years ago I was startled to come across a picture of him in the *Daily Telegraph* as captain of football at his prep school. The picture also included Ludovic Kennedy – the newspaper piece was about Ludovic Kennedy's early life.

It was towards the end of his time in prep school that Aunt Bee's authority over him was lost for ever.

I remember she said to Sprag, 'You are to do it at once.'

Sprag replied, 'I am not going to do it, and I can run faster than you can Aunty Bee, so you can't make me.'

I thought the heavens would fall, but Aunt Bee could see she was beaten. I was amazed at Sprag's temerity.

At one time Aunt Bee had a house on the Isle of Wight, but her stays were never long in one place as her neighbours were seldom on speaking terms with her. Going shopping with Aunt Bee was another of the horrors we had to endure. She would take us with her to the shops, and berate the poor girls behind the counter as 'impertinent upstarts'. We used to pretend we did not belong to her, and tried to hide under the counter as she was so desperately embarrassing. The family of children in residence when we were submitted to her rule were the Kayes, two girls and a boy, who had long since taken the measure of Aunt Bee and were undoubtedly disgusted to have two youthful additions to their lives. They must have quickly decided that they would control us as vigorously as Aunt Bee tried to control them. My first memory of them was their joint assurances to me, aged eight or so, that Australia was on the other side of the world where everyone walked on their heads. Australia, according to them, was not too far away and only required a powerful effort of will to reach it – which they said they often did. The mode of travel was to lie on the lawn under a rug and to will and will and wish oneself to Australia to see the marvels of those that walked on their heads. It would be hot passing through the centre of the earth but well worth it. Once arrived one merely wished oneself back again. As Mollie Kaye, later to become a well-known writer, was the ringleader of this trio, it is perhaps apparent that her powerful imagination and powers of persuasion were already at work. She told me in later years that her rose-coloured view of India, which led to her writing so many wonderful books, was fuelled by the desperate need that we all felt to escape from the rigours of life with Aunt Bee. Anyway at Mollie's instigation I lay upon the lawn under a rug and wished and wished and willed myself through to Australia. I got hotter and hotter and hopefully believed that the earth was beginning to swallow me up. Never once did I doubt the failure of this magic journey, which only reduced me to a sweltering heap, was any one's fault but mine – I had just not tried hard enough. So I tried and tried again so as not to let down the superior beings who had entrusted me with this wonderful secret of travel. After what seemed hours and hours and hours – and probably was – the Kaye family came to find me for lunch. They had completely forgotten the living heap on the lawn and expressed amazement to find me still there and no astonishment at all that I had not reached Australia. I recall that I was not so easily disposed of at other times.

The intervals between life with Aunt Bee were spent at the school, Oldfeld, in Swanage. The girls' dormitories were at one end of the school and the boys' at the other. The boys used to raid the girls' end, often led by my young brother and I was detailed to see them off. It happened all too frequently. I had Ruth Cadbury in my dormitory, who was very untidy. I also remember the beautiful blue banner over my bed: 'High endeavour is the inward light that keeps the path before us ever bright'. It may sound trite but it has been in my mind ever since as an excellent precept.

The Cadbury family, the well-known social reformers, who built the village of Bournville for their workers, sent three of their children to Oldfeld. Anthony, Brandon and Ruth. Their parents were concerned that many of the pupils had parents abroad who could not take them out for half term. So the good-hearted Cadbury parents used to collect all the children who were not going out a half term, and drive us over to nearby Studland Bay on the coast, where they gave us vast cream teas, a great treat after school fare, which had seemed to consist mostly of fried bread. Ruth Cadbury had a collection of beautiful silk dresses which we envied, as we mostly had cotton frocks. I remember that the Danish matron, Miss Quist, was horrified to find Ruth's dresses rolled up in bundles in drawers, instead of neatly hung in the cupboard, but she never succeeded in making Ruth tidy.

We sometimes spent blissful holidays on the school farm. It was at this school in Dorset and on its farm that I fell in love with the English countryside and the wonderful world of flowers that I found all around me.

The whole school regularly walked down to the sea to bathe in the summer through lanes of unforgettable changing pleasures. The meadowsweet and Queen Anne's lace scented the air above my head, we played with the buttercups, covering each other's chins and noses with pollen. The wild roses arched above us and as we reached the beach the mounds of sea thrift rustled in the salt breeze. We used to plod back, covered in salt after our bathe, to the old school buildings.

The school itself was a gaunt building on a hill not far from the sea, but to me it was set in paradise. Its garden walls, which we used to climb, were covered in pink and white valerian, which grew between the rocks of which it was built, and attracted multitudes of butterflies. Remembering this I have since tried in vain to grow valerian on the wall of my old rectory in Kent – so far with no success. It all remains a happy dream. To exiles I believe the delights of their homeland far exceed the pleasures of those who have never adventured away. Perhaps this underlies my vision.

From time to time Aunt Bee used to take little holidays from her self-imposed task of looking after other people's children. In retrospect it seems amazing to me that with a Quaker background she should choose to take holidays at Monte Carlo and enjoy a little flutter at the tables. This must have been her way of breaking away from her strict and probably gloomy life. For Monte Carlo evenings she wore a long red lace dress, complete with dangling diamanté earrings.

Her holidays meant fun for us as we always stayed with her cheerful sister Nora, quite different from Aunt Bee, and her husband Roddy and their children Pam and Paddy, at Maybush House. There actually was a large may bush beside the drive where we used to play hide and seek. It was a nice house with large stables and a tennis court set in its own fields just outside Southampton. This was wonderful freedom after Aunt Bee's furnished houses. Nora and Roddy also knew lots of people. Looking back I suppose they were mostly business people concerned with the port of Southampton. I know I used to enjoy going to stay with them from school, because as the train approached Southampton, there were dozens of coal trucks all painted with R. L. STEWART which I knew belonged to Uncle Roddy. I suppose off to coal some great liner. We played tennis and rode ponies, Uncle Roddy took us sailing from the Hamble, and we had specially good paperchases which took place all over Hampshire. These paperchases were organised by a collection of young people. Two leaders carried satchels full of torn paper which they scattered for us to follow, usually back to the house from which they had started.

I remember one occasion, when one of the leaders saw a large car coming, he started to jump about like a monkey. We all picked up sticks and began yelling and waving them about, pretending to be trying to catch him. The baffled car driver stopped and asked what on earth was going on. 'The monkey has escaped,' we said, 'we must catch it'; and we chased across the road where we all collapsed in a laughing heap on top of the 'monkey'.

We also had wonderful holidays at Campamento in Spain when we were very young. It was always a home from home for us, as it was where our grandparents had met and fallen in love. It was to see my grandfather and his sister Katherine, always known as Aunt Kay, that my father and mother and we children stopped at Gibraltar on our return from India in 1920.

I was four and a half, and my brother about eighteen months. Old grandfather Hugh was delighted with my brother, but I remember at lunch he sternly said to me, 'Little girls should be seen and *not* heard.'

Palm Tree House, where they lived in the village of Campamento, provided unexpected diversions. There were two maids, Bella and Pippa, and in the morning the goatherd brought his flock down the street. Bella and Pippa would run out with however many jugs were necessary into which the goatherd milked the frothing goats' milk. It was fun to watch. The other more gruesome affair was on the days that the pigs were killed. Their unavailing squeals were heard all up and down the street. Bella and Pippa again rushed out to collect the chitterlings.

There was another interesting ceremonial in which we all took part. My grandfather had to ascertain firstly that the wind was in the right direction. We all set to and washed dozens and dozens of bottles which dried out quickly if the wind was right. Then a huge cask of wine was rolled into the dining room, broached by my grandfather and quickly bottled and corked by the girls and laid on to trestles and into racks. It was an important affair so that all *had* to go right.

The great treat at Campamento was for all the children to be taken to the local potter. He had a special skill. He made 'pig' money boxes. They were made in the shape of a fat round pig with a slit in the top of the pig to put in coins. The pig's tummy had to be filled right up with coins – it was impossible to get them out through the slit, and you filled it until you could not get in another coin. At this point, and not before, you were allowed to have a ceremonial smashing of pig and to collect all the coins. It took a very long time to reach this exciting point. It was very tempting to smash the pig sooner, but was not allowed. Tony Innes once fell down the stone stairs and his pig smashed. We all helped him to collect the pile of coins, and a new pig was found for him.

Other memorable days were the special picnics to the cork woods. The coachman with his whip and smart hat would convey the grown ups, and the children used to ride in rope panniers on each side of a donkey. It was exciting but pretty uncomfortable and a return ride in the coach was sought after. The return was spectacular. The coachman, with help from all, had decorated his coach with flowers. He had flowers round his hat and a wreath of flowers round his whip. We wore garlands of flowers and flowers in our hair, and must have looked a charming sight. I suppose we must have been celebrating something like the arrival of spring.

I loved the life at Campamento, with all the fun on the beach as well. It was there I first fell madly in love. The Innes family were our playmates and they were there with dear old Uncle John the doctor and his wife Aunt Kitty who had looked after them since their mother died. The Innes family were John, Peter, Ruth and Tony. I thought Peter was absolutely wonderful, and I have a photograph of me firmly holding on to Peter (in the interval of building some magnificent sandcastle). He was all of eight years old I think, and I was five or six, and I had *no* intention of letting him go! Curiously, I recently attended his charming widow's eightieth birthday party, together with several of his remaining family.

5
'Finishing' and Africa

We had a happy time at school at Oldfeld in Dorset, and I was then sent on to a girls' school, Howells, in Wales. When I was at school in Wales I was confirmed by the Archbishop of Wales. I was bitterly disappointed that I had no great spiritual transformation – no beautiful dove descended upon my head, only the Archbishop tickled my hair. From then on I have found it hard to believe in God, but I have come to believe strongly in 'goodness' and to consider that the Christian faith is the best hope for humanity – although I do feel sad about the conflicting dogmas of the many Christian churches. At the end of my time at Howells the headmistress was determined I should go on to university – not so usual in those days. My mother was determined that I should not. She said she did not want a bluestocking daughter. What she really wanted was a 'social butterfly'. She won. I could quite see her point of view as she had been deprived of her children through all their schooling, only able to return for one holiday every eighteen months.

So having matriculated at sixteen, I left school at seventeen. My mother decided that her daughter needed 'finishing' before making her debut in India. A friend of hers in India was sending her daughter, another potential social butterfly, to a family in France, to get some French polish. My mother, I suspect to go one better, decided to send me to a finishing school in Paris. On arrival at Neuilly-sur-Seine, a suburb of Paris, we found that the school was in an apartment high up in a block of flats, with balconies overlooking the Seine and the street below. This little outfit was owned by Madame de Pellieux, a tubby French lady of aristocratic lineage (and, I'm sure, impeccable French) whose Christian name was Blanche. She was helped and organised by a much younger English woman,

Shelley Barker. They could accommodate up to six pupils in the apartment, and all our rooms were close together. The number of pupils fluctuated, as some were there for one, two or three months, or up to six months, which was to be the length of my stay.

When I arrived I found that there were two other English girls, one Russian and two Germans. Blanche and Shelley did their best for us. In the morning Shelley would give us lessons in French grammar. I shall never forget the delight with which she announced that one of her pupils had used the correct tense to catch a departing bus. 'Il faut que j'aille,' the pupil had said, and managed to get on the bus. We were given to understand that using the correct tense was the only reason for catching the bus.

In the evenings we had French reading and conversation with cosy Blanche de Pellieux, who tried to help us understand what we read to her. In addition, we had a visiting teacher who taught us diction. This was for the correct pronunciation of strange French words. Our lips and faces had to be actively elastic under her direction. She would make us say 'Le bébé a le nez épaté', forcing our lips to be extra active. She also had another sentence we had to repeat: it ended 'est sur le pelouse'. I can't remember what was on the lawn, but the 'ouse' was strongly exaggerated. We also had a visiting chaperone, detailed to take us to see the sights of Paris, particularly the Louvre. As we went down in the lift she used to say 'Draw nearer, mes jeunes filles, to listen to what I tell you.' Her breath smelled so strongly of garlic that we much preferred to back away. She always took us first to the Italian Primitives in the Louvre, and if any new girl was present, we went there again to start the new girl's education. As a result, as one of the longest-staying pupils, I must have visited the Italian Primitives about twenty times; they and the Mona Lisa became positively *vieux jeu*.

With so many nationalities at meals, very little French was spoken. 'Passez moi the butter s'il vous plaît' was about as far as we got, with German and Russian equivalents. At last the first term ended, and Blanche de Pellieux continued the instruction of her pupils at her cottage in the South of France at Murols in the

Auvergne. This was wonderful freedom after Paris, and there was swimming and boating on the little lake at Murols. I was the only pupil left by this time, and it was there I met Boris, a very handsome young Russian who actually had a car and offered to drive me everywhere; but this was quickly vetoed, although he was allowed to join me in swimming parties with the local French children and young people at the lake. These young people, far from admiring me as Boris professed to do, thought I was hilariously funny. My French speaking was a cause for huge mirth, so I quickly corrected it, and in the end became friendly with them all and they helped me with my French, although their accents may not have been very good. So after all the expense my parents must have incurred in Paris, it really was from these urchins in the Auvergne that I learned to understand and to speak reasonable French.

After briefly being 'finished', I decided I would like a career, and fancied I would like to be a journalist, another shock for my mother. She at last found a college called The Triangle in South Moulton Street in London, where they taught journalism and secretarial work. So there I went, for a few months, staying in digs in South Kensington. I learned laboriously to type. I wasn't much good at it but tried to reach a good speed. I had no time to learn shorthand, but learned speedwriting, which I later found useful.

It was while I was still in digs in South Kensington that Colonel Ian Burn-Murdoch, my godfather and an old friend and admirer of my mother, kindly decided to give me a good time in London. He had a flat in Artillery Mansions where he stayed when he wasn't on his estate in Perthshire. He took me to Quaglino's, the nightclub, where he fed me on so much caviare I could eat no more. Another haunt was the Savoy, where the wonderful Savoy Orpheans dance band played under Carroll Gibbons. We spent many happy evenings there, mixing with the *beau monde*. On one occasion, as we were foxtrotting around the floor, a heavy foot landed on my toe, and a male voice apologised profusely. It was Jack Hulbert. He and and his wife Cicely Courtneidge were just about the best-known entertainers of the day, and I was so thrilled that Jack

Hulbert had actually spoken to me, even though he had stood on my foot, that I must have dreamt of him for a week.

So with all this behind me, I set off at eighteen, with my parents, to India. I had very mixed feelings, as I had looked forward to studying English at university, or even becoming a journalist. My father had only been able to see us once in every three years. By that time he had become a senior government official in charge of the whole road network all over India. Much of it ran through princely states and he would travel around negotiating with different Rajahs for the road network to pass through their territories, coaxing quantities of rupees out of their exchequers. I went with my parents on several of these journeys.

Only a year after I arrived in India my mother developed cancer and my father had to take her home for medical treatment in England, where she stayed with her mother. She refused to take morphia. She was worried that her mind would be dulled during the little time she had left with my father. She sadly died soon after, while I was in Africa, where – after much consultation – it had been decided to send me to stay with Philip Mitchell, my father's brother.

Uncle Phil was then governor of Uganda. When I arrived in Nairobi on my way out there, I stayed at the Stanley Hotel. A page came up to me and said, 'Madam, at what time would you like your aeroplane?' I was eighteen at the time, and suitably impressed. The road to the airfield ran through grassland high above our heads, where we could hear lions grumbling from time to time. I was also amazed that, in those days, the grazing wildebeest had to chased off Nairobi airfield before the plane could leave.

We flew in a Tiger Moth, which Uncle Phil would use later while on duty, from his camp in the jungle. We flew over Lake Naivasha, where clouds and clouds of pink flamingoes filled the sky. I made friends with the pilot, who told me that he hoped never again to fly over nearby Lake Victoria. On the last occasion he had seen a cloud over the lake, and should have avoided it, because he had not real-ized it was the top of a waterspout. The lake water spins into the air, joining the cloud above, and rises to enormous heights. The pilot was caught in this, and was shot thousands of feet into the air. The aircraft controls froze. He had blood pouring out of his ears, and eventually he gained control, although the wings of the aircraft were holed with ice, and he had no engine. He managed to glide to the ground on the edge of Lake Victoria.

It was on Lake Victoria that I used to sail with Uncle Phil. We would also ride together through endless banana groves. I was told that one of the staple diets of the Africans was a porridge made from green bananas. I never tried it.

Once, when his wife was in South Africa, I went with Uncle Phil on a State Visit to the Kabaka (King) of Uganda. The Union Jack fluttered on the bonnet of our official Daimler as we were driven to the great cluster of huts in which lived the Kabaka with his family and followers. When we stopped and got out, 'God Save The King' was played while we stood at attention. These were the everyday conventions of Empire.

I used to ride such a lot with Uncle Phil, I expect he felt that I could do with more expertise, so he kindly gave me a present of spending a week at Molo, in the Kenya Highlands, with the Spencer Tryons. Spencer was a brilliant horseman, and so was his wife. They bred polo ponies in large numbers on their farm. The farmhouse was full of dozens of silver cups which they had both won at polo tournaments, and on other occasions. There were so many that I think his wife was too busy riding to have time to keep them clean and polished. They were all black.

The Tryons took pupils to improve their horsemanship, so there I learned a little dressage, and how to jump my horse over low fences. I even tried riding bareback, as well as later trying to play polo. Unusual then, for a lady. Polo is a very tough game; you ride off competitors in a pretty ruthless manner.

One day Spencer assembled two teams of ladies for a polo match. There were a few experienced players amongst us. One managed to smite the ball quite hard and we all cantered after it. Once we reached it, we had a sort of ladies' tea party, with most uncompetitive chat – 'Have you got the ball, Lucy? Do send it over here.'

[50]

One of the girls actually filched the ball out from among the ponies' hooves and managed to dribble it towards goal and we cantered after her (we never galloped, only cantered). I'm sure the match was an undignified tie, and it certainly wasn't high class polo. But it was fun to at least have had a go, if only to discover how difficult it really was.

While I was staying with Uncle Phil in Africa he had to go to the Great Exhibition in Johannesburg. He thought I would like to see it too. He had to fly down in a special aircraft, and I had to go by sea from Mombasa, calling at Zanzibar and Laurenço Marques on my way. Uncle Phil had asked a young friend of his to meet my ship at Zanzibar and to show me the island. When I reached Zanzibar I did not know that his young friend, being unable to meet me, had asked for a volunteer to 'meet the Governor's niece'. This volunteer met me on board, took me ashore, and drove me along the coast. He then asked if I would like a swim, and had I my swimsuit? I said that I had, so he said he had to go back to his flat to collect his swimming gear. We then drove through narrow streets and stopped at a great door covered in huge metal spikes.

'To stop the elephants charging,' he said. (There weren't any elephants in Zanzibar, but all the doors seemed to be covered in sharp spikes.)

He asked me to have a drink with him in his flat while he collected his gear. I knew Aunt Bee would have been shocked at my going to the flat of any young man, but I agreed, and we climbed up steep stairs of what seemed to be at least five storeys, to the door of his flat. He opened the door, showed me in, and closed the door. He then sat down and said,

'The door is locked behind you. You tell me that no one knows you're here, and you've walked into my trap. I'm a white slave trader, and I will have my dhow at the wharf tonight to carry you off to Arabia, from where you will never be heard of again.'

I was so shocked, I went to the window to see if I could jump out, but it looked certain death to do so, so I laughed.

He said 'I'm glad you laughed. From the look on your face at first, I thought you really believed me.'

I had been really frightened. I said I didn't want a swim, but must go back to the boat at once. He kept saying it had only been a joke, but I wanted no more to do with him; so down those long stairs we went and I was thankful to get out. We drove back through the narrow streets, then he stopped at a shop and came back with a parcel, which he put on my knee.

'A little present for you, to say I'm sorry,' he said.

I thanked him, but left it under the seat of the car as I got to the boat, and climbed the gangway. I stayed on board all the rest of the day, while the breezes, scented with cloves and spices which grew on the island, blew from the shore.

Months later, in Government House, Entebbe, my aunt was checking the incoming mail.

'Maxine,' she demanded. 'What man has been sending you a nightdress from Zanzibar?'

I explained my adventure, and later found that the young man was the son of a bishop and should have known better.

I had another adventure in Africa. I had a great friend in Entebbe, Phyllis Merrick, the daughter of the Chief Justice. She suggested we might get up a party to visit the Murchison Falls, also known as the Kabalonga Falls. This is the source of the Nile which thunders through a narrow gap from Lake Albert in a waterfall, one of the sights of Africa.

So we gathered together a party of young people, and set off in an old-fashioned paddle steamer across the lake to the falls. We all had cabins on this boat, which reminded me of the boat in the film *Sanders of the River*. As we approached the falls, we passed hundreds of hippos, standing in the water along the banks. They all seemed interested in us. When we reached the bottom of the falls, which were wonderful, there was even more activity in the water. Huge crocodiles seemed to enjoy having a shower under the falls, then drifting slowly down in the current, where they were carried along in front of the boat, against which they lashed their tails before disappearing down stream. Quite a sight. We enjoyed watching them in the evening light.

Early next morning we got up and prepared to go ashore to view the cascade again, from a different angle at the top. We had to pile into a small motorboat and a few had to wait for the next trip. When we were almost there we were nearly capsized by a hippo standing up beneath the boat. He must have been basking near the shore. Mercifully, the boat righted itself and we all hopped on shore as fast as we could. I had a new cine camera with me, which I had been given as a present. With us came a young African game scout, armed with a rifle, which made me realise we were in dangerous territory. All too true. After a dozen or so of us had walked up the narrow path beside the falls, we suddenly realised we'd walked right into a herd of elephants, which must have been drinking at the foot of the falls. I saw that there were wild elephants all around us, mothers and babies, and a huge bull elephant. This was very alarming, so everyone quickly left the path and scrambled up the cliff to one side to get out of the way. I was busy filming the elephants, and climbed the cliff beside the little game scout above the path.

The bull elephant, with trunk raised and trumpeting, charged down the path along which we had come. There we saw our friend Charles, a late comer, in white shirt and shorts, doing up the laces on his white tennis shoes on the path. We all yelled 'Elephant!' at him. He looked up and saw the elephant above him, and turned and sprinted as fast as he could back to the boat. I've never seen a fat man run faster.

Our shouts had attracted the elephant, and he swung round and charged at us on the cliff side. The game scout raised his rifle and fired, but the rifle did not work. He banged it on the ground twice; I stopped filming in fright. On the third go the rifle went off and the elephant fell at our feet with a hole in its head. Everyone on the cliff scrambled down to rush to the boat, but just then the elephant got to its feet again, and we all had to climb back up the cliff. The game scout raised his rifle once more, and this time it worked, putting more shots into the wounded elephant. Everyone fled past its body, back to the boat and on board safely. The next day, with the vultures gathering, the game scout cut off the dead elephant's tail, and presented it jointly to me and Phyllis. It was cut in half, and each of us kept a part of it for some time, as we understood that the tail of an elephant was supposed to bring good luck. We knew we were lucky to be alive.

6

Vanished Splendour

I returned to India from Africa in 1938 to care for my widower father, in both Delhi and Simla from where the Central Government of India worked. My father had a large bungalow in Delhi with a lovely garden. It had three large bedrooms, each with two bathrooms and a dressing room, and another detached flat beyond the porch: seven bathrooms in all. It had a large drawing room, a dining room, also large verandas which could be used as sitting rooms. The servants had a separate compound with their own apartments in their little village. As I remembered from Lahore, we had a large number of servants – really due to the Indian caste system. We had a head butler, called a *khitmatgar*, and his helper; a cook called *khansamah* and his *masalchi*, washer up; a sweeper who was very low caste who heated up the bath water in a primitive charcoal boiler – a *pipa* – and carried the buckets of hot water to the bathrooms for our tin tubs where we had only cold running water. We had to be careful to check that snakes had not crept up the drain into the cool of the bathroom. The sweeper fed the dogs and took them for walks, which the other servants could not defile themselves to do. We all had our personal servants or bearers. My father's bearer was called Hira Lal and I had an ayah, to look after me and my clothes. I hated her trying to brush my hair. We also had a house dhobi or washerman who used primitive methods of washing, beating the dirt out with stones.

Every day in Delhi the cook and his assistant would bicycle to the bazaar and back to buy food. Then they would prepare it, to be cooked on a charcoal brazier kept going by a large palm leaf fan. The cook was a lovely man. He would daily interview me to present his accounts in rupees and annas which I would settle and give him money towards the next day. He was scrupulously honest but it was understood that he would take '*dastur*' – a small mark-up for himself – as a matter of course.

These were our indoor staff. In addition, we had two or three gardeners called *malis*, a couple of grooms for our horses – called syces – and the driver of our car. They all had their families living with them in the compound, who did not always agree. We once had an old white-bearded *khitmatgar* who dyed his beard red with henna and took a new very young wife. A rash step. At times, amid screams, yells and thumps, her clothing would be thrown out over the compound wall while we presumed she was receiving a sound beating.

I was responsible for my father's servants and one day his bearer, Hira Lal, came to me and asked if we would take on his young brother as an extra bearer. I said we had quite enough already, but he explained that there was a desperate famine in his village, and that he would feed and house his brother if we could employ him. Of course we did so. Dealing with frequent famines was an important part of British government administration. Grain used to be sent from a prosperous area to a stricken one to feed the poor people. I think it would be true to say that there was no corruption. The grain for the needy and the money to help them did not go into the pockets of the Administration. I am afraid the same could not be said today. I have a photograph of a deputation waiting to see my father in his garden, asking for some favour I suppose. A basket of fruit would doubtless have held some bribe or valuable object which was of course returned or given to the Government.

My father also rented a house in Simla where the whole Government repaired for the hot weather. All Government files, all officials and their families and staff would go by a small train up the mountain to be unloaded by coolies. There we would all set up house again. Our single-storeyed house in Simla was like a large cottage. It was almost covered in a beautiful yellow Banksia rose. It had a lovely hillside garden, from which one looked out across the vast forested valleys towards the everlasting snows which stretched round the horizon.

In Simla only we either rode ponies or were carried by rickshaw.

We hired rickshaws – only rich Indians had their own liveried coolies. Of the coolies we used – usually peasant farmers from the surrounding mountainsides whose crops may have failed and who had walked into Simla to earn a few annas – many had TB. It used to upset my mother to be pushed up hills by men who were coughing their hearts out. She knew that she was more help to them by using a rickshaw than walking, as they thereby earned a little money, but it was always a source of great distress to her.

After my mother died my father, as a memorial to her, had a large solid waterproof building put up as a warm shelter for the rickshaw coolies who otherwise would have to have lived out in the open, with no protection. It is a building beside the church on the Mall in Simla. It would have pleased my mother.

One of the social centres in Simla was the Green Room over the theatre where amateur dramatics of a high standard were performed. Friends gathered there for coffee and drinks and it was rather like a club, with performances to packed audiences. Maybe it was the altitude of 6,000 feet which caused some emotional scenes. On one occasion the producer said to the leading lady 'You know you're no Venus.' The lady's husband was outraged, a punch-up with the producer followed, and he was sent 'down the hill' as a result. This meant banishment from the cool hills to the scorching plains for his misbehaviour.

The steep hillsides of Simla had many tennis courts where good games were enjoyed in spite of the altitude (my mother had been an outstanding tennis player). Most of us used to ride round 'Jacko' – the central hill on which Simla was built. Jacko was the abode of a troop of Langur monkeys who might start throwing fir cones at you if you were throwing sticks for your dog. These monkeys would jump from one tin-roofed house to another, making an awful din. They were otherwise harmless. There were riding picnics from Simla out to Carignano or Wild Flower Hall along roads edged with wild flowers, cosmos in great drifts, or flowering rhododendrons the size of small oak trees, while underneath might be carpets of lily of the valley.

[57]

Apart from outdoor life there was much entertaining – dinner parties, bridge parties and, I believe, poker parties, also weekly dances as well as the great annual Bachelors' Ball. The garden party at Viceregal Lodge was the main social event. All ladies would have worn long dresses, hats – probably large shady ones – long white gloves, and carried parasols. The men would either have worn uniform or morning coats, top hats and spats.

While all this social life seemed very light-hearted it was against a background of very hard work. About 3,000 British Government officials administered a country of 400 million people – an amazing achievement due in part at least to the Indians being naturally law-abiding but reflecting too the very high standards demanded of all British civil servants. A District Officer must often have felt lonely. He would ride round his district, which would have been of about 7 million people, with only his Indian staff. Sitting under a tree in the centre of the village he would administer justice in a foreign language and move on to the next village. When he returned to headquarters a social life with his family or friends must have made life so much more agreeable. So the wives, I think, made great efforts for their bungalows in the plains (never two-storied houses) to be as much like home as possible, and a busy social life was organised. The strenuous part was due to everyone's determination to keep fit. Men and women rode daily – usually in the early morning – competed in point-to-points, hunted the jackal, and the adventurous went pig sticking. We played tennis and squash, and some played polo. This was all against a background of threatened illness. Malaria – we all got it – was very debilitating; dysentery and typhoid were all continual threats to life.

The English community all over India kept strong social bonds in their clubs where games were played and dances held. Snooker was invented in a club in South India. Indians did not join the clubs, really because they could not permit their wives to do so. The wives at that time were all in purdah and never seen. We entertained many leading Indians in connection with my father's affairs but they never brought their wives. The very senior father of one of my

friends used to give tea parties for all the Indian children in his
office at which I used to help. This was quite a new idea. But there
were a few adventurous Indian ladies in the 1930s. The Maharani
of Cooch Behar, loaded with emeralds, could often be met dancing
with her Indian escort on Simla dance floors. But she was the
advance guard of the much later emancipated Indian ladies.

Aunt Bee's Quaker influence had remained with me, so that
when I arrived in India I was shocked at the life led by English
ladies there – it seemed to me to be non-stop amusement, bridge
parties, tennis parties, coffee mornings and frequent dances. Occasionally a few did good works helping at the YWCA to sell handicrafts made by poor Indian women. At that time very few ladies
had a working career – any work they did was voluntary. I believe
that their menfolk worked so hard and conscientiously for very
long hours running the vast subcontinent of India that the ladies for
the most part had to be left to their own devices.

Aunt Bee was adamant about what a lady should or should not
do; it was not ladylike to draw attention to oneself in any way. I
had to learn to behave as a lady which is why I suppose I had no
desire to be a 'social butterfly'. I did not know what I wanted but it
had to be worthwhile.

When I returned to India I was concerned that the women had
nothing useful to do other than housekeeping and caring for their
children. One lady was known to do her own cooking. Her
servants felt she demeaned herself as no other memsahib did such a
thing. The girls had a social life of games and parties and I, with no
alternatives, much enjoyed this. I seemed to collect a large number
of what we used to call 'boyfriends' and had several proposals of
marriage which I had no wish to accept. My poor father said on
one occasion, 'Do you know you have been out twenty-six nights
out of thirty this last month?' I remember I replied, 'My dear Pa, I
must have been slipping. What was I doing on the other four?'

Some friends once invited me to join them in a Christmas camp
out in the jungle, where we went by train. We seem to have celebrated Christmas by sitting on the engine. A tented camp had been

set up nearby, where villagers had complained that one of their buffaloes had been killed by a tiger. So on Christmas Eve my host and his daughter and I and another man set out in the evening to sit up in trees near the dead buffalo. The two men with their rifles climbed up into a machan – a little platform made from branches – in one tree, the girl and I, with no rifles, climbed into the other tree. We used very rickety ladders made, again, from branches. We had to sit absolutely still in the fading dusk, awaiting the return of the tiger to his kill.

I remember sitting watching the path to the kill in the deepening evening light and, to my amazement, in the path materialised – I did not see it come – an enormous leopard. My heart missed a beat as I knew that leopards climbed trees, which tigers didn't. My friend sitting beside me had not seen the leopard and nearly fell off the machan when there was a loud hard cough and heavy scratching below us on the trunk of our tree. I was quite terrified but had decided if the leopard climbed to attack us I would shine my torch to blind him and push my solar topee into his mouth! Mercifully he immediately moved off to the kill and in the dark lifted the leg of the buffalo to start a good meal. The men in the next tree heard this, turned on their torches attached to their rifles, and shot. The picture remains with me of a suddenly brilliantly illuminated leopard leaping over the fallen buffalo and then silence. After a long, long time the coolies arrived with ladders to get us down. Our men in the tree said they hoped they had killed the leopard, but were not sure. They climbed down their precarious ladder and one of them fell and broke his arm. We climbed down without mishap and, helping our wounded friend, walked in single file back to the camp. It was a mad thing to do – perhaps it was because it was Christmas Eve – as a wounded leopard might have killed any of us. But it was found dead the next morning beside the path on which we had walked.

On another occasion one of my friends asked me to go pig sticking with him. This is a *very* dangerous pastime. The wild boar are very large and devastated the crops of the villagers who were thankful to be rid of them. The boars take cover in very rocky countryside, covered in very tall grass, and are hard to spot. So they have an Indian lookout who rides a camel to get a better view. I arrived at the meet run by old General Armitage whom I knew. He was disgusted to see me. He said he didn't want young ladies as it was much too dangerous, and whatever I did I was not to fall off. 'Of course not, General,' I replied, whereupon my horse gave three smart bucks and landed me at his feet. I was embarrassed beyond words and thereafter rode well behind all the heats – though this was frightening enough in itself. The men with spears rode in several heats of four each in order to intercept the boar whichever way he jinked. After much galloping over very rough ground my friend decided he would like to ride my less exhausted horse and asked me to get up behind the lookout on the camel. He was a very, very smelly Indian and my only hope of staying on was to cling tightly round his waist. He soon spied a boar in the grass and as no spears were near he set off as fast as he could on the camel, calling the spears to follow. It was a mercy that I survived the day hanging on to this odorous Indian on a galloping camel. I was not tempted to try again. I am sure I was *not* asked!

My father did not take me as a single girl on tour with him and I had a full social life in Delhi. Our bungalow was very near the Club and here I played much squash and tennis and swam in the pool. The new swimming pool at the Gymkhana Club in Delhi had been opened by Lady Willingdon, who loved purple. She was the wife of the then Viceroy. She is said to have opened the pool in a purple bathing suit, accompanied by her many ADCs, all chanting 'Mauve qui peut.'

At home I had a few Urdu lessons so that I could talk to the servants and I used to go to the YWCA to help sell the handicrafts which had been taught to local Indian women. I also attended many dances.

On one occasion there was a fancy dress dance at the Gymkhana Club. I longed to go. There was just one dress shop in Delhi, which would not have stocked costumes for fancy dress. Most of my friends had Indian *derzis*, sitting crosslegged on their verandahs, making up costumes to their directions. I was naturally nimble with my needle and decided to make myself a costume as Alice in Wonderland. I used check cotton curtain material for the dress and cut up an old mosquito net to make a pretty frothy petticoat. I was pleased with my efforts. As a result I was invited by the Viceroy's daughter Joan and the Viceroy's staff to join them at the Black Hearts Ball in Simla all as characters out of Alice in Wonderland.

The Black Hearts Ball, sometimes called the Bachelors' Ball, was organised and given by all the Delhi and Simla bachelors. They wore scarlet cloaks over their evening dress tails and white waist-coats, with large black hearts stitched on to the cloaks. This was their thank-you for all the entertainment they had received from married families, and was one of the highlights of the Simla social season.

On the occasion of my first Black Hearts Ball – dressed as Alice in Wonderland – I was invited to open the Ball with the Viceroy, Lord Linlithgow, dancing the State Lancers. This was a great honour, as his partner was always supposed to be the 'Nicest Girl in Simla'. (I think this title was probably bestowed on me that year by the Viceroy's Military Secretary, an old friend of mine.) It was also a great responsibility, as the State Lancers was a complicated dance. It was danced by the Viceroy's party only, while everyone else watched. We had to have a serious practice beforehand, at Vice Regal Lodge, during which the Viceroy complained to his Military Secretary that his partner kept going round the wrong way. The Military Secretary replied that it was His Excellency who had to go the other way about. So I did not have to correct him myself.

I had many friends on the Viceroy's staff, not only Pat Southby, an ADC, who was my second cousin and the grandson of Juliet Garton, but several others, including Philip Nash, the Viceroy's Private Secretary, and George Burns, his Chief ADC. George was in the Coldstream Guards and was my chief dancing partner. Whenever a waltz was struck up George would catch my eye and we would move on to the dance floor together. He used to take me out duck shooting all round Delhi, and we had endless picnics together. George was one of the party when we all went to the Black Hearts' Ball together, dressed as characters in Alice in Wonderland. I was Alice, and George came as the White Rabbit, with a wonderful brocade waistcoat. White Rabbit was always fussing over the time, and White Rabbit, alias George, took out of his waistcoat pocket a huge gold watch, very thickly studded with diamonds and other gems, to check the time. It was a fantastic piece of jewellery, and made me realise how enormously wealthy George must be. He later became, I think, the most popular Colonel of the Coldstream Guards that they'd ever had. I loved dancing with him.

Lord and Lady Linlithgow were an impressive pair, both tall. They held annual investitures, which I attended in Viceroy's House, New Delhi when my father was twice knighted. These were, and were intended to be, very splendid occasions. The Viceroy and his Lady, both dressed in cloth of gold or silver, and covered in jewels and decorations, sat on a dais on gilded thrones. At their feet sat several young Indian princes, all dressed too in gold or silver brocades. They had turbans of gauze with egret feathers in diamond clasps, carried jewelled daggers and wore necklaces of precious stones. All the Indian princes and rajahs were also present and magnificently dressed. I remember meeting the Maharajah of Patiala who was particularly impressive. He was a very tall large man and was wearing what seemed to be a complete breastplate of pearls and diamonds. It's a recollection from a lost age.

When I was in Delhi I attended many occasions, balls, investitures and garden parties at the Viceroy's House – surely Lutyens's masterpiece. It had wonderful water gardens at the back with flagstone paths and long pools, with their water lilies and low, illuminated fountains. On state occasions guests could wander through these amazing gardens. The only problem was that if you were curtseying to the Vicereine as she passed by, you had to be careful not to step backwards into the water behind you.

The last time I went there was for the marriage of the Viceroy's daughter – Lady Anne Hope – to Pat Southby. His mother was

Phyllis Southby, my Quaker great-aunt Juliet's daughter and first cousin of my mother. She and her husband Sir Archibald Southby lived in beautiful Burford Priory. Their son Pat was serving as ADC to the Viceroy when he got engaged to the Viceroy's daughter Anne.

I walked up the grand stone stairway to the Reception past the men of the Viceroy's bodyguard, resplendent in their scarlet tunics, gold sashes, enormous puggarees and tall boots, who with their lances and pennants lined every turn of the stairs. They stood so still at attention they seemed like waxworks, and I was almost overwhelmed with the splendour of the occasion.

After the Reception the bride and groom drove off in an open carriage from the front of the Viceroy's House, with the men of the Viceroy's Bodyguard riding ahead of and behind the carriage. I remember watching the cavalcade of scarlet coats and flying pennants as it disappeared down the slope through the great gilded gates for its ceremonial drive down Kingsway – it was an unforgettable sight.

The author as a baby, with her mother

Early transport

The author's parents, Kenneth and Lilian Mitchell

Kenneth Amyot Mitchell, 'Sprag', the author's brother

Lenare studio portrait of the author, 1938

Major-General Sir Philip Mitchell

The Maharajah of Patiala

Bill and Maxine Magan married in New Delhi, 30 November 1940

The Cuckoobird catalogue

St Michael's, 'the old rectory', drawing by author

Castletown, Co. Kilkenny – watercolour by author

Parterre, Castletown

The author's husband, Bill Magan, on the occasion of their Diamond Wedding

7
War and Marriage

While I was in India war was declared, which changed all our lives. The day after it was declared I rode the ten miles from Wild Flower Hall, the hotel where I was staying for the weekend, very fast into Simla to Army Headquarters. I left my horse with a red-coated peon at the entrance. I knocked on the door which bore the name-board of a friend of mine. He looked up at me in horror and asked what on earth I thought I was doing in Army Headquarters, where no ladies were ever seen. I explained I had come to offer my services in *any* capacity. He replied that Headquarters was more than adequately staffed by Indian male clerks and that young ladies were definitely not required. I was very upset but cheered up when my old friend Ouvry Roberts, the Deputy Director of Military Intelligence, who later became a very distinguished general, telephoned me to say that he had heard I had been thrown out of AHQ – all Simla had heard, I said – but would I like to be his private, private secretary? I was, of course, delighted and worked in Military Intelligence for several years after that.

It is curious to remember that at the time the fact that I had taken a course in journalism and secretarial work just before I went to India (giving my mother another shock) was not considered socially desirable, and one Colonel's lady was heard to remark that it was not quite the thing that Maxine knew how to type. However, all soon changed and many more girls went to work at AHQ, thereby freeing men to go off to war. Indeed the Viceroy's daughter Joan asked me for a job in my office – I had to turn her down. When my husband to be, Bill Magan, wrote a note that reached the C-in-C suggesting many officers' jobs could be taken by the well-educated daughters of officers and officials, he was told that he was 'an impractical visionary'.

The Military Intelligence work I was being given under Ouvry Roberts's aegis was receiving and collating reports from two agents in Bombay and Karachi. I had to put all the information under separate headings including one called 'Bazaar Rumours'. It was mostly news of shipping movements, not really relevant to the war in Europe. If these constituted the only intelligence received by the military, I thought they were very inadequate. I was concerned that they should be far more comprehensive. Meanwhile I continued running the agents, finding as much other useful work as I could in my office.

My brother Sprag was up at Oxford at the time. He wrote to me in India to say that he wanted to go into the Army – not into the Colonial Service as his father had wanted. So I wrote back suggesting that he came out to India to discuss his future with our father. This he did, as it happened just before war was declared, when he immediately joined up as a Gunner in the 125 Field Regiment R.A.

We saw him off to join his regiment. He went to the Middle East where he took part in all the major desert battles and did well. He was finally captured by the Italians and was in an Italian prisoner of war camp near Arno. Just as the Allies were successfully invading Italy he and a great friend decided to try to escape. Sprag, my companion from my earliest years, was shot dead but his friend escaped. We were informed by telegram. For me and my father it was a cruel and desperate loss.

Early in the war my father was put in charge of all petrol rationing, transport and American Lend-Lease to India. I could no longer be chauffeur-driven to my office in the huge Secretariat Buildings which we called 'Baker's Ovens' (the architect, Sir Herbert Baker, came from Kent). As I could not be seen to use even so much as an egg-cup full of my father's petrol, I had to use a pony and trap. As a wartime gesture the Government no longer moved up to Simla in the summer but remained working in the heat of Delhi. So in a temperature of 120° Fahrenheit I would drive to and from my *not* air-conditioned office for my lunch in this pony and trap. The heat was so intense that it seemed to bounce off the ground. I used to have a brief siesta at home after lunch and would return to the office to find all my colleagues fast asleep on their desks.

I was happy as a civilian in AHQ but the day came when all civilians had to get into uniform and become military personnel. I became a staff captain with three pips on my shoulder, and had to learn to salute – from a friend in my office who had been a grocer in civilian life. On my first day in uniform I was walking across one of the large open quadrangles of Baker's Ovens when I spied emerging from the far door a red-tabbed general who was an old friend of mine. It was now or never, and as we drew abreast I treated him to my best new military salute. This seemed to throw him completely, and in astonished accents he said, at nine in the morning under a brassy Indian sky, 'Oh, er, good afternoon, my dear!'

At this time Lady Linlithgow decided to review all the ladies newly in uniform in Delhi. As her Rolls-Royce drew up at the old fort where all the girls were on parade, she stepped out to inspect us, followed by her ADC, a tall young man in pale blue viceregal uniform, to whom she handed her feather boa. As she walked down the ranks, he followed her, carrying the feather boa, the only man on the parade ground.

At the Imperial Delhi Gymkhana Club I was introduced to Bill Magan. He was staying with Vernon and Viola Bayley, old friends of mine. Before the war Bill had been selected from his regiment for intelligence training at the Intelligence Bureau in Delhi. I confided in Bill my anxieties about the limitations of our own reports. He said I was quite right. 'Your lot are just amateurs,' he said, 'who have started up a little intelligence agency for Ouvry's own interest. Of course there are professionals. The Intelligence Bureau works closely with MI5, the Security Service in London. They cover the world, and will inform the Indian Government about any important developments.'

Bill's Intelligence Reports on very serious matters were sent to my office and it was my duty to take them to Commander-in-Chief's Military Secretary, Bunny Careless, who was another friend of mine. Bill's reports were so strikingly different from others I received that I used to withdraw into the ladies' cloaks on my way to the C-in-C to read them – which I was quite entitled to do. One of his reports, on a mutiny in an Indian Cavalry regiment, began: 'Sobha Singh sat slumped in his chair in the middle of his cell, under a bare electric light bulb.' I couldn't wait to read on, to learn that Sobha Singh was a Moscow-trained Communist agitator and a very dangerous man.

I thought that Bill was an outstanding person. Not only were his intelligence reports brilliant and often amusing, he was a superb horseman and he used to do wonderful treks into the Himalayas to find out about the country, in which none of my other friends seemed interested.

He told me that on one of his Himalayan treks, when he and his porters had camped just below the snow line of the High Himalayas, he was struck down with a bad relapse of malaria. He suffered from severe rigors, and the sweat froze on his body in his tent. His porters and muleteers thought he was dying, and could have left him there. But after a few days Bill struggled weakly to his feet to survey the path ahead. He found they were camped beside a small river, and the path continued on the other side. The snow above had fallen into the river, but there remained a bridge of snow over the torrent. The only alternative to crossing this snow bridge was to climb 3,000 feet to the hard snow above, and to cross above the source of the river. Bill knew that he was not able to climb 3,000 feet, so he said to his men, 'If I lead a laden mule across the snow bridge, will you follow?' They must have thought he was mad, but agreed. Bill then led his mule across the snow bridge, which was shaking above the rushing torrent, and reached the other side. All his ten muleteers followed him safely across the river. As they looked back, the snow bridge collapsed just after the last mule had crossed.

Bill said, 'Sick men should not make dangerous decisions,' but it was just as well that on this occasion this one did, or he would never have returned from those mountains. He then rode one of his mules back down to the Kulu valley, where he recuperated before returning to Delhi.

Bill whipped in to the Delhi hounds of which I was a humble follower. The previous winter he had been given permission to act as a Master of the South West Meath Hounds in Ireland for a season. His aunt was the hunt secretary and the Hunt had invited him. The adjutant of his regiment in India was amazed when his Colonel agreed to Bill continuing his leave for the whole winter, and said so. His colonel replied, 'I consider that being an MFH qualifies you for horse management, man management and financial management – all very important training for a cavalry officer.'

So Bill was allowed to have a very successful winter's hunting in Ireland. This was in his family's tradition – his mother's father, Assheton Biddulph, had owned and hunted the Queen's County Hounds in Ireland for most of his life and his mother had always ridden close to her father since she was a young girl and was an excellent horsewoman.

Bill's mother Kathleen was a gallant lady. When she was living at Killyon Manor in County Meath, his family home, the IRA Troubles were at their height. Large houses belonging to Protestants were being burnt down all over the country. Bill's family was a Protestant landowning family, and had at one time thirteen large estates, stretching from one side of Ireland to the other. One of their great houses, Clonearl, had already been burnt down by the Rebels.

Kathleen Magan was going out hunting one day, and as she walked down the stairs, her whip in one hand, the front door burst open, and in rushed a pack of IRA, intent on burning the house down. Kathleen was outraged. Small and neat, whip in hand, she said they had no business coming to the front door, and ordered them to go to the back door at once, and state their business. Astonishingly, they shuffled off and the house survived.

Bill and I used to ride together every day in the early mornings – often round the Delhi Racecourse. I had decided that Bill was outstandingly the best of my many boyfriends and the man I would really like to marry, so one day I took my courage in both hands and told him so. He replied that much as he would like to reciprocate he was unable to do so as he was already engaged to the daughter of an Irish peer who had wanted him to marry her when he was Master of the South West Meath Hounds in Ireland.

A few weeks later I had a letter from Bill saying that the Irish girl had broken off their engagement for the duration of the war, and that he hoped I was still of the same mind as before. Apparently he had a worrying time since I took a while to think it all over again, but of course I was very happy to agree in the end.

We were due to be married in the Cathedral Church, New Delhi, on 30 November 1940. The day before, Bill told a friend of his, Ross Howman, in his office, that he was feeling very ill. Ross told him not to worry as it was only wedding nerves, and that he had felt the same. Bill went home early and found he had a temperature of 103. He was suffering from a severe relapse of malaria. We were to be married by the Bishop of Lahore, an old friend of my father. He came to see us the evening before we were to be married, at the Baileys' house where Bill was staying, and we explained about the high temperature and relapse of malaria. The Bishop was very cheerful and told us not to worry. He explained that recently he had married a young officer who had travelled down from the North West Frontier and was so tired that he 'fell asleep in the sun'. As a result he got severe sunstroke and as the Bishop started the marriage service he fainted and collapsed at the feet of his bride. They both picked him up and, as the bride propped up the bridegroom, the Bishop continued to conduct the marriage service as fast as he could. Then both of them collapsed and the Bishop had to hold them both up while he carried on with the service. By the time he had completed it they all lay collapsed on the floor together. The young man recovered and the couple told the Bishop how grateful they were for his support and speedy marriage service. 'So,' said the Bishop, 'you can be assured that you can rely on me.'

So we did. Bill got to the church on time and insisted on wearing his new tall leather boots which had not been 'broken down'. As a result, every time he knelt down, the boots cut him behind the knees, causing him great pain, making him shoot forward. However, he looked very handsome in his uniform and tall polished boots, even with a temperature of 103. I took his arm and we left the church together under an arch of crossed lances sent by Hodson's Horse to make a guard of honour for us. Now with myself at nearly ninety, and with Bill at ninety-eight, I can truly say that we have lived Happily Ever After.

Philip Nash, the Viceroy's Private Secretary, was on home leave at the time of the Bachelors' Ball. On his return from leave he stopped at Cape Town, where he met a mutual friend and told her that he was returning to India intending to marry Maxine. The friend told him he was too late as she had just got married to Bill Magan.

My Uncle Phil was attending a Delhi Conference at the time on how Africa could help India in the war against the Japanese, and so he made the speech at our wedding. We are still in touch with two of our bridesmaids.

After Bill had recovered from malaria we spent a blissful honeymoon in Kulu – a small village in the Himalayan foothills. Bill used to consider it civilisation when he arrived there on trek from the outer High Himalayas, but it was rather lacking in amenities. Once arrived we had to drive back down the valley for about fifty miles to be able to buy bread, rice or tea – anything in fact – so we had to stock up with all we might need. Our little house did have a bathroom with a tin tub, but as I sat in this bathtub, I could see through the wide gap between walls and roof, where a foot of snow and icicles were hanging from the roof. The bathing did not take long! But it was such a beautiful place, I could not resist trying to paint the rushing river and the snowy mountains all round. Bill reckoned he could draw too – which he could – and so started us on our lifelong painting holidays together.

Our first home in Delhi was in a 'tented camp', erected to provide wartime accommodation. It was three large tents in a row. The end tent had a built-in brick fireplace where we could light a good fire, and was our sitting room; the central tent was divided into a dining room and a bathroom, and the third tent was our bedroom. The kitchen quarters were in a separate small tent behind the dining area. It was in fact very comfortable and when Bill's old friend Miles Smeeton came to stay with us, sleeping in our sitting room, he found it much more comfortable than where he had slept on one of his many adventures with Bee, his intrepid explorer wife. She had once walked across China alone, saying she was studying the food. When the British Consulate warned her of the dangers she would encounter in the Chinese interior, she replied, 'It's quite all right. I far prefer dishonour to death.' In fact, she placed herself in the care of the women as she approached each village and walked the length of China unharmed. She walked across China long before Peter Fleming wrote of his travels in *News from Tartary*.

After a while my father asked us to return to share his large house and to help him look after several paying guests he was putting up when they were posted to Delhi and had to find wartime accommodation. These included Alan Roger, our lifelong friend. Their arrival, all with their personal servants, made our servants' quarters even more congested.

We both worked in Military Intelligence, but Bill was soon sent off on duty. He has written his side of the story in his book *Middle Eastern Approaches*. He has told in it of interesting and adventurous times capturing German spies in the Persian mountains, who were trying to disrupt our wartime aid to Russia. He touched on our great sorrow in losing our dear eldest son Thomas from dysentery, and my losing my dear brother. Thomas had been born in 1941, and when he was two years old, it being far too hot for him to stay in Delhi, I had sent him and his nanny to the cool of the mountains in Kashmir. On their return journey, she allowed him to play with a block of ice in the railway compartment, put there to keep them cool. But the ice had probably been made from infected water, full of disease. Our little Thomas, on return to Delhi, developed serious dysentery. There are two strains: only one was discovered and treated, the other never diagnosed, and from this he so sadly died. He was buried in Delhi, and I have returned twice to see his grave.

While we were in Delhi our second son George was born in 1946. He had a problem growth at the base of his spine – similar to cancer. The Delhi doctor who operated told us that he had not been completely successful in removing the growth, and advised that I should fly him home for further treatment. I decided to take him to Bill's family in Ireland, rather than to war-ravaged England. We decided that the quickest way to go was by a new Sunderland flying boat from Karachi. After the Persian Gulf our first stop was Cairo, and we landed on the Nile with the city lights stretching away on both sides. The next stop was Sicily, in very rough seas. So rough that we were thankful to get on dry land for a while. Seats were so scarce on the seaplane that I had to withdraw to the back, behind a curtain, where a pile of mail bags provided a place for me to feed my tiny baby. Once in Ireland, the Dublin doctors were able to perform a successful operation on him and, thankfully, he had no further problems with his spine thereafter.

While Bill was away on duty in the Middle East, and my father was not on tour, I often stayed with some of his friends. One of them was B. J. Gould, the British Resident in Sikkim, who invited us to spend Christmas with him at the Residency at Gangtok in Sikkim. This was on the borders of Tibet and Bhutan. The young princess of Bhutan used to visit the Sikkim Residency, and was pleased to meet another girl, so I invited her to come for walks with me. She seemed doubtful, but we went on several walks together. On one occasion one of the local Bhutanese saw her, stopped and prostrated himself on the ground before her. He apparently said that as the daughter of the Rajah she had no business to walk around the country unattended; she should have had a bodyguard, and that I must be a bad example as I had been seen walking about alone. I think she felt we must discontinue our walks, but she did come with me to see a local performance of Tibetan devil dancers. These dancers came from the temple and had long brass horns through which they made a hollow trumpeting noise, while circulating slowly in their golden robes around the arena. Tibetan tea

was passed around the audience in tiny bowls. I drank mine rapidly
out of politeness, and the Residency doctor tapped me on the
shoulder and said 'Go slow. Green tea is mixed with rancid butter,
and each bowl acts like a dose of salts.' Thereafter, I only sipped it.
By the end of the performance I'm sure all the devils were trum-
peted away.

One day B. J. told me that we might be expecting some American
airmen to stay. He explained that now America was helping India
against the Japanese, one aircraft flying from India to the Assam
frontier, where the Japanese were trying to invade India, had turned
north instead of east, and had actually flown into Tibet and crash-
landed onto the Tibetan plateau. They ended up riding mules back
to India. So one day outside the Residency I saw a bunch of American airmen saying farewell to their mounts. They kicked the mules,
saying they never wanted to see them again, and let them loose. I
think their bottoms must have been very sore after such a long ride
from Lhasa. They had purchased enormous Tibetan headdresses,
necklaces of lapus lazuli, and tall fur-lined boots. They obviously
fancied their getup a lot. As we were having them to stay, the butler
looked after them, and we were told we would meet them in the
dining room, with its polished table, silver candelabra and crystal,
which looked wonderful, and was probably something quite
strange to the young airmen.

When I came down to dinner, before my father, I was in real
trouble. These men had not seen a white girl for months, so I was
chased round and round the dining room table, which had to stop
on the entrance of B. J., who lived in some state. He had the equiv-
alent of a butler and two footmen on his Sikkimese staff, who
served a four-course dinner. During dinner, the airmen told us of
their adventures. They reckoned their compass had gone wrong on
leaving India, and had caused them fly north and not east to Assam,
and they had been amazed to see the Himalayas high up in front of
their aircraft. As they had no more fuel, they had crash-landed on
the Tibetan plateau. They had no idea where they were, and threatened the local Tibetans with the guns they all carried. However, the

[74]

Mount Ephraim House

Summer Garden Party

SATURDAY 15TH JULY 2017 • 2-4pm

'A watercolour' by Anne Keller

Mega Plant & Cuttings Sale, Grand Raffle, Coconut Shy,
Residents Craft Stall, Tea & Homemade Cakes, Live Music

Come along and join in the fun!

greensleeves
care
You're among friends

RSVP to: Karen Cooper
01892 520316 | karen.cooper@greensleeves.org.uk
Mount Ephraim House, Mount Ephraim, Tunbridge Wells, TN4 8BU

Registered charity no. 1060478

local Tibetans were good to them, fed them and gave them quantities of Chinese brandy, before helping them on their way to Lhasa, the Tibetan capital.

'That goddamned Potala,' said one. The sight of this had so overwhelmed him that he could not believe it was true, and thought he was suffering from an illusion brought on by the Chinese brandy. It was in fact the vast Potala Palace in Lhasa with its hundreds of windows. The Tibetans feasted them in Lhasa for a week before the airmen decided they must return to India, and they were given mules to ride.

After dinner together at the Residency, we finished dessert, and everyone was given a glass bowl of water with flower petals floating in it, in order to rinse our fingers.

'This bowl's got me buffaloed. Do I drink it?' asked my neighbouring airman.

We explained, and sent them all to bed. Next day they wanted to go to Calcutta. I said the bus didn't go so far that day.

'It sure will,' said one, 'I pack a heater.'

All the airmen carried guns. Poor bus driver.

While I was staying with B. J., he invited me to stay on with him in Sikkim, and then to accompany him as secretary on the forthcoming British Mission to Lhasa, of which he would be the Head of Delegation. The purpose of the delegation was to meet the Dalai Lama, with whom the British had a treaty, to discuss Tibetan affairs.

I was strongly tempted, but replied that I had a wartime job in Intelligence in Delhi, to which I had to return. I would have been so interested to go, to learn more of these amazing spiritual people. I had heard that some of the lamas were said to have a race from all round Tibet. These lamas were locked in small rooms with very small windows, pointing in the direction of Lhasa. Their spirits were said to race to the Potala, in Lhasa, and the winner was recognised and acclaimed by all the people. The winner never arrived in person, only in spirit, but was cheered by all. Hard to comprehend, and I would love to have learned more. Alas this British delegation was probably the last to visit Lhasa before the Chinese invaded and took over Tibet, causing the Dalai Lama to flee.

Once I stayed with Sir Frederick Tymms and his wife Millie. He was the Director of Civil Aviation for India, and invited me to join them on his trip to open the first airport in Jaipur. The first night in Jaipur we dined in the Maharajah's famous Lalique dining room. It had pale grey velvet walls, a pale grey carpet and chairs and beautiful Lalique glass wall lamps in the shape of fantailed peacocks. The table was black plate glass with a centre panel lit from below of two peacocks with long tails. Each plate, and glass, was a fantailed peacock – all in soft moon-coloured Lalique glass. It was a dream, and I learned later that it is all now in a museum.

The main dinner given by the Maharajah was held at a vast long mahogany table with silver bowls of red roses down the centre – only reached from each side with billiard cues. After dinner we adjourned to the ballroom. The Maharajah should have opened the ball with my friend Millie. But I suppose I caught his eye and he asked me to open the ball with him.

I was taken by Sir Frederick and Millie to Kashmir to have a holiday on a houseboat. We were poled up through lakes edged with iris in full bloom. They also took me on a trek into the Kashmir mountains to Sonemerg. We pitched our tents where the snow had melted and crocus were blooming, a pale mauve colour with golden stamens opening to the sun as the snow melted around them. A sight few people can have seen. All our equipment was carried on ponies and our bearer served us meals outside our tents. I started to sketch the amazing scenery. I think Kashmir with its lakes and snow-covered mountains is the most beautiful place I have ever been to in the world.

While in Kashmir, we had heard that a tribe of Kazaks had crossed the Himalayas into India. We decided to go up into the mountains to meet them. We found the tribe, from Kazakstan, in Outer Mongolia. They had decided to emigrate to avoid Communist Moscow rule and were making their way to Calcutta, of which they'd heard wonderful tales. The passes in the High Himalayas can only be used in the height of summer when the snowfields have melted. Several hundred of these intrepid Kazaks with their small ponies and dwarf cattle had crossed one of the passes into India, but many had failed to get through. They were grazing their little cattle on the mountainsides when we walked up to see them. They found us as interesting as we found them, in their brightly coloured costumes. We usually had an interpreter to help us understand them. I soon had a cluster of Kazak women around me. I was startled as one by one they came up to me to pull at my legs, and walked off roaring with laughter. I had never seen a Kazak lady before, and none of them had ever seen nylon stockings. It kept them laughing for hours.

Early in the war Millie Tymms was made the head of the Red Cross in India. She organised parties of volunteers to supply hospital needs for wounded soldiers. I drew posters for her to attract volunteers, and they were displayed in the Simla Green Room and in the Delhi Club, saying 'KNIT FOR OUR SOLDIERS AND SEW FOR OUR WOUNDED'.

In New Delhi Millie's volunteer force worked in an office in Connaught Circus, the main shopping centre. She took some of her faithful servants to help. They had worked happily for her for years.

In India there had always been severe communal troubles which the British Government kept under control with its excellent Indian police force and loyal Indian troops. Troublemakers may have hoped that while the British Government's preoccupation was with war in Europe, this could have given an opportunity for communal troubles to start again.

One day Millie was going home to lunch after a morning's work in her Red Cross office. Her Muslim servant walked out in front of her carrying a heavy tray of bandages. A Sikh on a bicycle, with his large *kirpan* (a Sikh sabre) on his handlebars, dismounted, swung his *kirpan*, and swept off the head of Millie's Muslim servant, whose body fell at her feet. The Sikh took up some bandages to clean his *kirpan* and cycled off. There were no police near enough to catch him.

8

Egypt

When Dick White, the head of MI5, MI6 and Intelligence Adviser to the Cabinet, came to see Bill in Delhi, he would have known of Bill's Intelligence background, which I had not understood. When we were first married in Delhi, every single night, between one and two in the morning, Bill would put on his large black cavalry cloak which covered him completely to the ground, and disappear into the hot night. He never appeared again until a late breakfast, and I never asked where he had been. I knew he must have been on duty. Dick, though, would have known that every night Bill drove to a cottage in the garden of the Viceroy's house, where he and Malcolm Johnston, a friend in the Indian police with a radio operator, were nightly in touch with German Intelligence in Berlin. Bill and Malcolm called themselves an 'Indian Communist Revolutionary Organisation', and said they were determined to undermine British rule. They gave the German Command some true, and much very misleading, information. The Germans passed all this 'revolutionary' information to the Japanese in due course, enabling the British to be in touch with Japanese Intelligence, and capture Japanese spies as they landed in India. After Dick's visit, Bill was invited to join the Security Service (MI5) as head of the office in Jerusalem, Palestine, which was in the throes of the Jewish Rebellion. After a very demanding time there, Bill was posted to Egypt to take over as head of Security Intelligence Middle East in Cairo instead of Alec Keller who had become ill from strain.

Security Intelligence Middle East soon afterwards moved with Army Headquarters Middle East from Cairo to Fayid in the Suez Canal Zone in Egypt, where Bill was allotted a large tin bungalow in what was known as 'Red Flannel Alley' as it was inhabited by all the top brass in the British military and naval world then in the Middle East.

This was the first time he had been able to have his family with him and I joined him there with our two boys, George aged five and Hugh aged four, and their nanny. The first impression was of wonderful weather – lovely sunny days when we looked out across the Great Bitter Lake through which all the Suez Canal traffic used to pass: daily we saw the stream of vessels of all sizes passing through, from liners to tugs, together with elegant Egyptian feluccas and small sailing dinghies raced by intrepid local sailors from the garrison force. All our dwellings in the desert appeared to be of very poor quality – all that could be thrown together at brief notice, I expect, to house the British influx – but they withstood brilliant sunshine and the occasional *khamsins* – the desert sand storms that actually stripped the paint off any buildings or vehicles in their path. There was virtually no rain, but the English love of gardening was supported by irrigation from waters of the Nile, which must have been full of rich and questionable nourishment, as all plants grew like mad. The wisteria I planted used to grow several inches a day and soon quite covered our tin bungalow. Our boys loved digging in the sand and swimming in the Bitter Lake and their nanny started a little nursery school, which became very popular.

Bill's staff was quite large. We felt we were a home from home for them and did what we could to make them feel part of the 'office family'. They could all play tennis and swim; there was sailing on the Lake and there were more sophisticated amusements at the French Club in Ismailia where Bill's deputy David Stewart and his wife Bobby were living. There was a lot of to-ing and fro-ing up the road lined with casuarinas and palm trees on the edge of the Lake to Ismailia and back to Fayid, where we lived.

There were also occasional jaunts for Bill and me across a hundred miles of desert to Cairo on business. This could have been very boring but our companions on these trips were usually George Munn from Military Intelligence and David Ingram from Naval Intelligence who both had marvellous funds of funny stories, and together with Bill's Irish stories we used to laugh all the way to Cairo and all the way back.

Mollie Kaye (who had been responsible for causing me to lie under a rug and wish myself to Australia) had also been posted to Fayid with her husband Goff Hamilton, now a major-general. Goff, as a very young officer in the 'Guides', had won a DSO on the North West Frontier of India. On return to Ireland he had been acclaimed as a gallant hero, and married the heiress to Blarney Castle. She accompanied him back to India but decided she would prefer him to join the Irish Guards. He replied that Hamiltons had always been in the 'Guides', and returned to India without her. He later met and married Mollie Kaye. They were very hard up to begin with, as on a major's pay he had to pay alimony to the Lady of Blarney Castle – which she hardly needed. So Mollie tried to make a little money to help support their two daughters, and started writing books and painting pictures. She asked me to go to Cyprus with her to paint pictures to sell in an exhibition on our return to Egypt to raise some cash.

When we arrived there we were met by a wild Cypriot taxi driver. He drove us recklessly across Cyprus to Nicosia. Mollie said if she had not felt so seasick after our journey from Egypt on the deck of the boat (to save money), she would have died of fright. Mollie and I then left Nicosia for Kyrenia in our little hired car, to go as paying guests with dear Mrs Wu. This lady's husband had 'shaken the Pagoda Tree' in Shanghai, returned loaded with trea-sures, had been taken ill and died in Cyprus on his way home. Mrs Wu was left with a house full of fantastic Chinese works of art and very little money and was forced to take in paying guests. Her Chinese works of art were so valuable that even King Farouk had travelled from Egypt to buy some pieces.

One day, as we drew some pieces of Mrs Wu's beautiful Chinese jade and lacquer, we had a telephone call from Nicosia to say that Bill was coming from Cyprus to join us, but that his aircraft was on fire over the Mediterranean. When I told Mollie she rushed to tele-phone the office in Nicosia to ask if the message had come from Egypt and if Bill had safely returned there. No one knew. Mollie brightly told me all was well and we went out painting. She kept

hearing aircraft taking off and thought these were probably search-
ing for Bill in the sea. However, Bill had returned to Egypt with his
aircraft engine on fire and fire engines racing down the runway
beside them. The next day, in the same aircraft (the best of a bad
lot, he was told), he reached Cyprus to be treated to the same
lunatic driving by the same Cypriot taxi driver, who drove him to
Nicosia, where we met him.

While we were out painting, Moll decided to write one of her
thrillers – this was called *Death in Cyprus*. She asked me what the
Secret Service would do, as she thought this must be what Bill was
doing. I said that those who knew could not say, and nobody else
knew anyway, so she could do as she liked. Eventually she wrote
that I was pushed off the top of St Hilarion by the villain, a gun
runner, but was saved by my long hair catching in the bushes, from
where I was rescued by Bill – the hero. The book became one of a
series of her thrillers. Mollie and I returned to Egypt, where we held
a very successful exhibition of our paintings. Everyone liked to
have a painting of Cyprus, the holiday island.

I had always enjoyed drawing and sketching and a little group of
us used to go off painting to different parts of the Canal area. The
group included a bishop, Mollie Kaye, the Countess of Bandon, who
was very skilful professionally with dried flowers, and several others.

One day we decided to paint the rows of flame trees in Ismailia,
all reflected in the small sweet water canal. They were beautiful.
Unfortunately the Egyptian police decided to arrest us. We were
hauled off to the police station and informed that we must be spies
as we were drawing the bridge over the canal so that Israeli aero-
planes could come and 'go boom-boom'. It was quite a struggle to
prove our innocence and to get freed.

Bill always liked to keep fit and he used to go for brisk walks
across the desert and always carried a walking stick. As this always
sank into the sand at every step I asked him what was the point of
taking it. 'To keep the girls off, of course,' said Bill. I knew he was
popular with his staff but I thought this was overstating the case!

We used to have parties for the girls and families. Sometimes we had limerick parties. Everyone was given the first line of a limerick and had to make up the rest. There were some very amusing results, but I can only remember one:

> There once was an AQMG [Assistant Quartermaster General]
> Who, when singing, could get up to C.
> When he sang in the choir,
> He got higher and higher,
> But burst when he got up to P.

Because I was always concerned to look after the families both in Egypt and in England, some forty years after this I was invited to become an Honorary Member of the Security Services Society for former members of staff. This meant I have been able to attend the twice-yearly lunches at which the Director General speaks to all retired officers, and keeps them informed of the latest situation. A privilege for me.

Our main party of the year in Egypt was our annual Christmas party. We invited all the staff who had no better engagements to Christmas dinner with us. We suspected that many made a point of having no other engagements that night. So we all dressed up – thirty-two or so of us – and squashed into our tin bungalow. The Sudanese servants (*suffragis*) entered into the fun. On the occasion of one Christmas party they asked me for two torches to use in the kitchen. I presumed they must have been looking for mice or something. However when the moment came the two *suffragis* marched in with a pair of turkeys held shoulder high with scarlet lights coming from their bottoms (torches covered in red paper). To round off the meal the flaming plum puddings were laced with brandy butter brightened up by pink cochineal.

These were some of the lighter moments against a background of very hard work during unsettled times. We were in Egypt for three and a half years and during this period the only time that Bill took off was Christmas afternoons. I must admit that I occasionally grumbled, but we had a good life.

9
The Old Rectory

When we all got back to England from Egypt, Mollie and Goff Hamilton invited me to go on a painting trip with them in Spain. Goff wanted to take his Aunt May, an excellent painter, for a holiday. She was in her late seventies. So off we started on the long journey. We drove across France and over the Pyrenees to Madrid, where we stopped to look at paintings in the Prado. Then on to Granada via Toledo, where we stayed in a Spanish *posada* just beside the Alhambra Palace, the wonderful architectural master-piece of Moorish art, dating back to the fourteenth century. Its Generalife Gardens with hundreds of fountains playing in a long pool are a delight. After a stop there, we drove to the coast, where we sat on the beach, painting and viewing the Rock of Gibraltar from the north.

Later Goff drove us on to the smugglers' hilltop town of Ronda, built literally on top of a precipice. By this time we had produced a great deal of work between us and were ready to go home. Goff thought dear Aunt May was too frail (she was so confused she thought we were still in Toledo), and that she would not be strong enough to stand up to a long return journey home in his old estate car. We put her on an aeroplane in Gibraltar to fly back to Ireland. He parcelled up her beautiful canvases to prevent them sticking to each other, or to us, as they bounced about in the back of his car, and we three drove the long way home.

A few months later I had to visit Ireland, and I decided to call on Aunt May at her lovely old Irish house near Dublin. She was delighted to see me, and told me that she and her sister had been in dire trouble.

'When I got back from Spain, I was told something had happened that we'd never had before. We had an overdraft.'

Eva her sister had crashed her car, and the insurance money had helped. So Aunt May had herself wrapped up in rugs and was driven down to Punchestown Races, where she painted racehorses to sell to Americans and to pay off the overdraft, which she did. She was so pleased. Little did she realise that both she and her sister, who had studied under Orpen, would later become celebrated Irish painters. Aunt May's best works, signed L.M.H. for Letitia May Hamilton, are now quite valuable.

On our return to England for Bill to take up his appointment as Overseas Director of MI5 we had to decide where to live. Bill would have to commute to the West End daily. It soon became clear that Bill's job was not sufficiently well paid by the Government for us to be able to educate our children as we wished. So, as I considered Bill's job to be very worthwhile, I suggested that I should try to find some work 'on the side' to help the family finances. As my father had recently retired from India to Suffolk and started a little fruit farm to augment his pension, I decided I could learn about fruit from his fruit adviser and grow fruit myself. It would have the advantage of my being able to work at home and not to leave my boys, and would earn some extra money. So we got the advice of an excellent man from Seabrook's fruit farms in Suffolk, and when we found various properties which were in easy reach of London for Bill's work, discussed with him their suitability for fruit growing. We eventually found an old rectory in Kent with good access to a station for travel to London, but I thought it was too large and costly to run.

'Nonsense,' said Bill, 'it's only a potty little rectory.' (He had the idea of his Irish landowning family's mansions in his head.) Our fruit adviser said that we *must* buy it as it had good soil on a splendid southern slope and would be ideal for fruit growing. Our London bank, where we had our savings, was not very helpful and finally advised us to buy the rectory on a mortgage. We did this through our old solicitors, and had great pleasure paying it off after a very few years.

When we finally settled down at St Michael's, we found that

having friendly local cricket matches was a good way to get to know our neighbours and their families. Our friends Helen and Den Campbell, who lived at Underriver House, had an ideal little cricket field and pavilion at Underriver. We used to have cricket teas and matches there for as many boys as we could collect. They were fun, and the nursery, I'm sure, for many budding batsmen. We played on other village cricket pitches all over Kent, and the families, parents and sisters used to enjoy watching their sons and brothers playing, batting, catching and dropping catches.

Later on George and Hugh did very well at Winchester. Hugh was opening bat. The games master came up to me at a match and told me that this must be my finest hour (I think he didn't realise I really knew nothing about cricket). And George was a very successful spin bowler.

After they left school, Hugh went to work overseas with a company building roads and airfields all over the world. He was a very attractive character, but could never achieve his ambitions, because sadly he developed severe schizophrenia. After years of battling with this agonising illness, he took his own life; something of course which I can never forget. I now work tirelessly for charities which help mental health. Poor, poor Hugh.

George had got a 'remove' at Winchester every term. But when he left school we told him that we had to sell the last of the Magan Irish estates in order to afford to live in our grey stone rectory, as we could not afford to run two homes. He was distressed.

'What? Sell Killyon and the hidden diamonds?' he said.

We said we had to. We knew that Bill's great Aunt Augusta had owned a famous necklace, with diamonds reputed to be the size of pigeon's eggs. One day she was said to have turned all the workers off the place and hidden the diamonds. School holidays at Killyon had been happily spent hunting for the diamonds. On one occasion Bill's sister Maureen had caught her foot in a hole in the field, and further investigation revealed a casket, which she thought must contain the diamonds. She rushed into the house with the casket, only to reveal the bones of a dog. No one living locally has ever become suddenly rich, so we think they have never been found. So George said he refused to go to university, which he was more than able to do, and decided to go at once to work in the City, in order to make enough money to buy another family home in Ireland. We were happy with his decision.

By 1954 we had finally achieved my mother's dream home, an old greystone house with a cedar tree outside an English village. At the time we bought it, I remember I drove to the top of the hill at Wrotham overlooking all Kent, and said in a loud voice with no one to hear 'Kent, here I come.' I did not know what I was going to do but I was going to do something good. In fact what the house meant was work. Our new home was sold to us by a builder who was not very tidy. When he left, all his carpets – such as they were – were still nailed to the floors. Those that we could not possibly use we had to haul up physically, absolutely full of nails and dust, and we had to ask him to cart them away. We then looked at the walls, which were all very shabby. They all needed wallpaper or paint. Again with no money to spare, we decided to do what we could to the house and garden ourselves. The boys had to be taken daily to their kindergarten, Hilden Oaks in Tonbridge, but Bill had a little time before he had to start making the daily journey to London.

Helping Bill to wallpaper a bedroom meant that at one point I found myself draped in a large soggy sheet of glued paper which tried to stick to me and not to the wall. So we decided instead to paint the dining room; we had a board stretched across two trestles which Bill mounted daily while I tried to work in the garden. He was painting the dining room ceiling and it seemed to me to be going *very* slowly, so I came in from the garden and offered to help him. I climbed on to the trestle with my tin of paint in my hand. I painted the ceiling above my head with skill and speed and told Bill what I was doing. Alas it is a truism that 'Pride goes before a fall'. I was standing on the narrow board and had painted a large area above my head when I stepped backwards to continue my work. I thought I had stepped back on to the board, but alas the board was not there. I had stepped into thin air. My pot of paint swung round in an arc pouring the contents over all the tools and equipment on the floor while I hit the floor with a crash, covered in paint. Bill started wearily cleaning up the mess and made no inquiries as to whether I was bruised or had broken a leg. He only said he would prefer me not to help him another time – it took too long. I had to agree.

The pleasant and final result of green painted walls and ceiling became a very good background for the collection of tapestries we rescued from Killyon in Ireland. These had been worked by ladies of the family. One was unfinished. The lady's husband, William Henry Magan, is supposed to have strangled her before she had completed it. There is a large empty gap on the canvas, with the initials WHM below.

Another large tapestry is of the sack of Basing in the Civil War. It shows the old Marquess of Winchester, with whom Bill's family had a connection, in great distress at the Cromwellian soldiers looting his treasures. A small boy is in the background being bribed to give away secrets. There had been a dead body in the original picture which the stitching ladies did not want to include. The drinking soldier originally had his foot on the body. The foot is now only raised.

The other tapestries were reputed to fall off the wall when a family member died. So far they have remained comfortably in place.

At the time we collected tapestries, we decided to bring over what furniture we could use from Ireland. There was a collection of carved furniture, made in 1810. Two very large mahogany benches, topped with carved boars' heads, and a set of matching mahogany chairs, again topped with the heads of boars. Not comfortable, but handsome, and which we now use all over the house. The mahogany benches, which had been used in the ballroom at Killyon, were much too large to use in our old rectory. One took up most of the hall, so we used them in the garden instead. I know that this treatment did them no good, and eventually George had them restored, and is using them in his wonderful Irish house, where they are more in scale with their surroundings and look very impressive. This is at Carrick on Suir in the South of Ireland. George had done brilliantly in the City, jointly founding a merchant bank with Rupert Hambro, which they eventually sold to Nat West Bank for a very large sum of money, his part of which was more than enough to buy one of the finest mansions in Ireland, Castletown Cox, much grander than Killyon Manor had ever been. It is now called Castletown House, and George has spent the last twenty years or so renovating, decorating and furnishing it, and improving the gardens.

Other pieces of furniture we brought over have proved very useful and look very good when polished. For the rest of our furnishings I went to the salerooms and auctions to get what I could as cheaply as possible. When I bought four iron bedsteads, the assistant asked if I was starting a school. I explained they were only for the family. We tried to get comfortable divans for friends.

We had a collection of family portraits on the walls. I had them cleaned, and frames painted white, which made them look more cheerful. They are nice little pieces of history, going back to 1610. One of the most interesting is an enormous watercolour portrait of William Henry Magan the Youngest, born in 1819. He looks magnificent in uniform, with a colourful sabretache. He became an equerry to Queen Victoria, and used to ride behind her carriage. On one occasion the Prince Edward, later Edward the Seventh, was sitting in front of the Queen in the carriage in fits of laughter and giggles. Queen Victoria looked back over her shoulder and saw William Henry, her equerry, making funny faces at the young prince. 'Ride back, sir,' she said. From that day on, equerries have to ride at a distance from the royal carriage, so that such *lèse-majesté* cannot recur.

While we were setting up house Moll and Goff gave us some house-warming presents. He painted a pair of beautiful green glass decanters for us with the Magan coat of arms. This had a shield with three boars and a chevron topped by a ferocious boars head

'Couped, Tusked and Bristled'. Moll painted two little vignettes of Kulu with bright colours on black paper; again, they have given us much pleasure over the years. Much later, after dear Aunt May had died and left everything to Goff, he gave us half a dozen of the paintings left in her studio, which she had not sold. Some lovely work, and some not so good, but all marvellous to have. They have now been returned to Ireland, where they were painted, to hang in George's house.

When we had collected a few pieces of furniture, we gave little supper parties for friends old and new, to come to our new home. We also gave a few limerick parties, as we used to do in Egypt. One contribution was referring to our new home in Seven Mile Lane in Kent. It was:

> A bald head from Seven Mile Lane,
> Who longed to get hairy again,
> Bought a full-bottomed wig,
> Several sizes too big,
> And to shrink it
> Went out in the rain.

10

The Fruits of Our Labour

We knew nothing at all about fruit when we arrived at St Michael's, except that apples grew on trees. Our fruit adviser said it made more sense to pick fruit from the ground, rather than climb up trees. So we planted three and a half thousand head-high trees. It took years for them to come into bearing, so with four acres planted with dwarf apple trees, I planted the remaining four acres with strawberries.

I then visited Covent Garden market, to discuss marketing my crops. The salesmen there were grim-looking men who said they had no wish to market anything I grew, as 'fruit was overdone'. This was a nasty shock until I met dear Jim Stead, the director of the firm of Pouparts, who was most helpful. He said marketing fruit and vegetables was difficult, but advised me to grow something different from other growers. He suggested I grow alpine strawberries, called fraises des bois on the market. We were most successful with these for years, until they developed a severe attack of phytophera, the same damp-induced disease that had caused the potato blight famine in Ireland. After this first outbreak, we planted our strawberries on ridges to avoid the damp, and were able to get one pound a pound for them – riches to us.

Jim Stead was always helpful, and told me of a poor lettuce grower whom he frequently advised to pack his lettuces tighter in their crates. Eventually no more lettuces arrived and Jim said he heard that the poor grower had been committed to the local mental hospital muttering 'Tighter … Tighter … Tighter.'

'Fraises' were usually red but occasionally they were white and tasted just as good or better than the rest. I had them packed separately and called them 'Swiss Whites'. One day Pouparts returned my 'Swiss Whites' and said that their buyer did not like them as they did not taste as good as the red.

'Please tell your buyer that they taste just as good and the buyer does not know what he is talking about,' I said.

'As they were returned from Buckingham Palace, you will have to accept their decision and not argue,' Pouparts said.

On another occasion Pouparts's man telephoned me on a pouring wet day.

'How are your fraises getting on? We're expecting a delivery from you tomorrow.'

'I have six ladies out in the field picking fraises under umbrellas,' I said.

He replied, 'I'm glad to hear it. Tomorrow the Shah of Persia is giving a banquet for the Queen Mother who loves fraises and they are on the menu.'

We dried them all carefully in bath towels before filling the little punnets and making the delivery.

We also had half an acre or so of raspberry canes – again the fruit was very easy to pick and we did well with them. One sunny morning on coming downstairs, Bill looked at the barometer.

'It has gone through the bottom,' he said. 'We should be due a hurricane.'

I hoped he was wrong. But for the first time the chickens refused to come out of the henhouse. The pickers all arrived in their straw hats with their picking baskets belted round their waists and had started to pick when the hurricane hit us – the raspberries were turned into raspberry jam and our lovely cedar tree lost most of its branches in the garden. At least the chickens came out of the henhouse. It was a disaster, we had to have the rest of the cedar tree cut down. The garden looked very empty without it and we could only hope for a better crop of raspberries on their new growths next year.

In the midst of all the hard work of picking, packing and marketing, I took a day off for the arrival of our youngest son James, who was born in our old rectory in 1957. Our Christmas card that year showed James in his little carrycot, wrapped in a shawl, with, tucked around him, punnets of fraises, strawberries, corn cobs and apples, and called 'Harvest 1957'.

It was such a joy to have this little chap growing up, running around the garden and playing games with us and his brothers. He played chess with his father from his earliest years. He was known as Jamie to everyone, and loved rides to the fields in the wheelbarrow, and attempting to pick the brightly coloured tulips. We had to persuade him to admire and not to pick them. He was such a bright boy: he won a scholarship to Cambridge from Winchester and read medieval languages. He was also adventurous, and joined the Greenjackets, as he admired his soldier father. He was soldiering with them as adjutant, in Wales, when he heard of the tragic death of his brother Hugh, to whom he'd been very close. As a result, he converted to Catholicism, and worked with Mother Teresa for many years after – a great comfort and solace to him in the religious life in which he happily continues.

I used to get fruit pickers whom I knew from the village. Our local policeman, PC Pimp, used to enjoy coming up to pick with the girls. He used to bicycle up our hill past St Michael's cottage where the Attwoods lived. One day as he puffed past Frank Attwood digging in his garden, he called, 'Do you think, Frank, that the Great Train Robbers have hidden their swag in St Michael's churchyard?'

"Do you think, PC Pimp, that I'd be digging my own garden if I did?' said Frank. I believe the swag was never found.

One day I had a telephone call from a woman in the village. 'I hear you need more pickers,' she said. I agreed to take her on the next day although I did not know her. When she arrived I realised I had made a mistake, she must have weighed all of fifteen stone. Each time she knelt down to pick the fruit she completely squashed the row on which she was working, and a fair proportion of the rows on both sides of her. The girls were having a good laugh, and not only at the new arrival. Dear Mrs Bell had sat on a wasps' nest and needed first aid as a result. Mrs Bell was a punter, always betting on the dogs. She recognised a bad day when she saw one.

I was fond of all my pickers but only employed them for a couple of months or so in the summer. They asked me if I could find some winter work for them, which I could not do at the time. I gave them a little extra work with another cash crop – this was the edible maize or sweetcorn, which we picked when they were very young and so good to eat. We slid the cobs into our picking bags, and they always seemed to me like slippery fish. They were a useful crop and we enjoyed eating them grilled with melted butter.

11
Cottage Industry

In Bill's job as an Overseas Director of the Security Service he had to visit his outposts. This meant travelling to Australia and the Far East to go round the world from east to west, starting in America where he had colleagues to meet. He had a cousin in California, Dr Wellesley Magan, and his wife Katherine, and so we decided to go there together. I would stay with them while Bill went on round the world.

Wellesley was a very successful doctor, who had a clinic in Covina, a suburb of San Francisco. He never kept patients waiting, as the 'delay went right back to the parking lot'. His grandfather, Percy Magan, had sent his eldest son Percy to study ranching in California. The young Percy had not enjoyed this but he made great friends with some Seventh Day Adventist medical missionaries who were kind to him. He joined them and eventually helped to found Loma Linda Medical University in Palm Springs, California where there is a 'Magan Hall' to this day. He later married Dr Lillian Ehrmann, a nutritionist. This was in a farming area. Local farmers by the name of Kellogg were also Seventh Day Adventists. One day they said to Dr Lillian that they grew acres of maize to feed cattle and they only wished it could be used for human consumption. Dr Lillian worked on this and invented the 'corn flake'. It made so much money for the Kelloggs they offered to pay her a large fee, which as a medical missionary she would not accept, but all the travel of Percy and Lilian was paid for by the Kelloggs, and they travelled in style. Someone in the family said, 'If there were silk pants going, Poppa had them.'

While I was in America with them, Wellesley and Katherine decided they should show me something of the American way of life. They took me to nearby Disneyland of which, as Seventh Day

Adventists, they did not really approve, but I loved seeing it all. We then walked from one end of Disneyland to the other, looking at all the shows, and looking in vain for a stall from which to buy our lunch, with Wellesley saying that no way would he pay more than 95 cents each for our hamburgers. He decided they were all robbers and took us back home to Covina to have home-made hamburgers in his kitchen. However, in far from penny-pinching mode, they drove me down to see the Grand Canyon, where they had arranged for me to have the best and (most costly) hotel bedroom overlooking the canyon and the Colorado river.

On the way there we drove through Salt Lake City, Mormon territory, where they pointed out that every house had two front doors, one for each wife. We also drove through Monument Valley, which they said was the Great Divide of America. I said that curiously it was my great divide too – my fiftieth birthday. and memorable that I should arrive on this day. We stopped at a shack in Monument Valley which was used as a regular film location. The opulence of the cuisine was more Hollywood than the premises. We were ushered to a table, and a vast cake with fifty candles was brought in. Everyone in the shack, film stars included, rose to their feet and sang 'Happy Birthday'.

We stopped later to picnic in Red Rocks Canyon where I did my best to paint the red rocks reflected in the water. A pair of Americans with a caravan, who spent their retirement drawing and painting around America, said Red Rocks Canyon was one of the finest places they had painted.

Grandfather Percy died in 1947. A friend said of him 'Percy Magan was born, and has been at all times, a gentleman.' We became very fond of the family, especially of Margie, Percy's granddaughter, who married Judge Walter Allen. After he died Margie developed a successful interior decorating business. We all last met at a service at Loma Linda University, in a hall which holds a thousand people seated as in a theatre. They have three services daily.

Before we left for California, all the papers were saying that Britain had to export goods to live. We should all 'Back Britain' by exporting. I thought my pippins and fraises were hardly likely to put us on the trading map, but went happily off to California to see what else they might want from Britain. When I got there I found that all the Americans we met seemed to live in great comfort and elegance. I noticed they used quantities of linen, even on the floor, where they had heavy linen druggets. Of course they had linen sheets, towels, and table cloths. Linen was hung on their walls, as well as being used as covers on chairs and sofas. I looked for labels and found it was all imported from Belgium. On my return to the UK I bravely visited the head of a large Irish linen firm, Ulster Weavers, and said I thought they were missing a real opportunity in California. The reply, from their grand office in London, was that they used to have fabric designers, but the management had disagreed with and dismissed most of the designers, and since the loss of the designers the Belgians had taken all their business.

It stuck in my mind that 'design sells'. So I then paid a visit to the Design Centre, recently set up in the Haymarket, where I saw many well-designed objects – chiefly toys. One thing that caught my eye was a scarlet bag on a coat-hanger for holding laundry or toys, designed as an English letterbox with black felt lettering stitched on. I thought this item could be a souvenir for 'Backing Britain'. I felt goods of this sort would attract foreign currency even if they were not exported. So I met Peggy Brown, the maker, in a teashop in Heal's, to see if we could work together, (her son came too, to make sure I was respectable). Peggy said she could not personally stitch hundreds of bags, and it would be cheaper to have the bags printed with no felt letters. So my next adventure was to Todmorden in Lancashire to a lovely old building on a mill stream where fabric printing was done by hand. The printing was done by colour rolled on to the cloth in different patterns with different rollers for each colour. The manager was not very keen to see me when I asked if he could print a few letterbox bags for me. He said he would need volume, at least a few hundred, or maybe other designs as well. So I decided to see what else I could do to have a go at 'backing

Britain'. We later used Tiviot Prints, run by the ever-helpful Taylor family at Broadbottom in Stockport.

Peggy said I could use her design if I paid her a royalty to which I agreed. I thought I should have a range of bags with a British theme. So together with the letterbox, I had a British lion, designed by Ken Townsend, a Punch and Judy and a Guardsman, designed by Jan Pienkowski. These were the designs I had to start with. I found the designers through the Design Centre and they later became friends for life. Once printed I had the bags stitched up in the village of East Peckham by an expert seamstress, Elsie Huber, who taught me a great deal. She explained that skilful stitching is done by the fingers lightly pulling and stretching the fabric through the machine for difficult places. My work on bags would not be difficult: quite straightforward work that any girl using her own home sewing machine could manage, but Elsie could always deal with any real stitching problems.

My four bags once made, I had to try to sell them. I had no idea how to do this. I had once met Arthur Stewart Liberty, as his son Richard was at Winchester with our son George. So I got an appointment to see Arthur Stewart Liberty at Liberty's in London. When I arrived in his office he said I'd made a big mistake in asking to see him. The shop had independent buyers in every department who used their own judgement and didn't not take his advice. 'I could have an aunt making string vests and she might want them to be sold here, but I would have to ask the buyer in the right department who would probably refuse them. I can't ask them to sell something they thought unsuitable.' 'Anyway,' he went on, seeing me looking somewhat downcast, 'I've asked my Merchandise Manager to find you wandering in the street, not knowing where to go. He's just coming in and will take you to the right department.'

So I was conducted to the Gift Department in Liberty's and the buyer ordered a couple each of my bags. I had hoped for a much larger order, but the buyer was taking no risks. An order for eight bags was not exactly volume for the printer, so I had to try other places. Off I went to Heal's who ordered a few more, and I got a small order from Selfridge's too and a little one from Fenwick's. So I was in business. I took the risk of ordering fifty of each bag from the printer, and Elsie stitched up my first orders. But again I was in trouble. I had no idea what to charge. I had asked the buyers what they would pay and agreed, with no idea of what they cost me, as I was so pleased to have got started.

A friend said 'You *must* have an accountant.' It was a daunting thought but I got hold of a local man called Mr Blumer. He sat in front of me putting his fingers together. 'You've made every mistake in the book, said Mr Blumer, 'made a bloomer in fact. Before you start, you *must* carefully cost everything: the cost of cloth, the cost of printing, the cost of cutting, the cost of dispatch. When added up you add 10% for your overheads and finally 100% for profit and reinvestment.'

It sounded very daunting and almost stopped me going on, but it seemed feeble to stop and I was delighted when I saw one of my bags hanging in Liberty's window. So I did my sums, raised my prices which the buyers kindly accepted, and planned what else to produce.

I had a neighbour, Michael Montague, living in nearby Roydon Hall, who was Director of the British Council for Exports to Asia at that time. I showed him my bags one day and then he telephoned me. 'I have a delegation of buyers from Japan in this country,' he said, 'and I have made an appointment for you to show them your bags tomorrow morning at 10 am in the Design Centre in London.' 'I can't do that,' I said, 'my business is only me and it has no name.' 'By 10 am tomorrow you must have a name that no one else could have used,' said Michael. I rushed back to Bill and said please write down as many silly names that you can think of for my business that nobody else could have used or have wanted. He made a list. I chose 'Cuckoobird', and we were sure that no other business was called by this name or could want it. So the next morning I met some Japanese gentlemen who seemed to whistle through their teeth. Bowing to me said they would be interested in being Cuckoobird's agent for Japan. This was beyond my wildest dreams and so

I told my neighbour, as I hoped it must lead to good business. So what else should I do?

I now had an Indian fabric importer in Manchester, a fabric printer in Lancashire and stitchers in Kent (some friends of my old fruit pickers). So I set up a system. I decided what objects I was going to try to sell to 'Back Britain'. Once I had the idea, I made up the shapes myself and once I was pleased with what they looked like, I laid them out flat and asked a designer to design the patterns for them in as few colours as possible (for economy). Once designed they were printed in Lancashire, then sent back to Kent in rolls of cloth. Then came the organisation of cutting out each object in dozens, and putting the parts together with zips, cottons or whatever else was needed. Plastic bags full of these were taken by a supervisor – another old fruit picker – to the stitchers in their homes in the village of East Peckham and round about, and returned to our home completed. As this was all brought to a spare bedroom it became a problem to manage. My son George, by then an accountant, said he had 'never before known a business where the workers worked both on and under the table'.

Later still, I had office staff to house too, a girl to type invoices, a secretary to write my letters and a packer to parcel up and send off the goods. So I then had to take possession of my old disused stable block, where there were stairs to a hayloft from which the hay was thrown down to the horses. The hayloft was where we installed Elsie Huber to stitch up our samples, and we transferred all our cutting and packaging into what used to be an old stone hen house. My office had once been a home for the rector's pony trap, and outside was a brick slope where the pony trap used to be wheeled out and washed down in the yard. It was all full of character but started to be a tight squeeze.

When I decided to make souvenir lavender bags, I found I could get lavender in quantity from Norfolk but it was cheaper from France and Spain. First of all I made lavender dolls hanging by ribbons. I called my first little lot 'Cries of London'. They were so pretty and successful I found I needed literally tons of lavender to fill them, and it was cheaper to import in bulk. So with 'Perfumes from Provence' in mind I flew to Nice in the South of France where the bulk of the lavender was grown. I drove to the fields above Nice where they had sacks and sacks of lavender. My French friend with me tested each sack. 'Poof! No good, too much stalk,' he said of the first sack, and we finally decided on a sack with the most powerful scent and no stalks. This was loaded on to our little car which would not start, so after paying for the sackful of scent, we were pushed off by half a dozen cheering lavender growers and drove back to the airport at Nice. I had to pass this sack through the Customs. The officials in pale blue coats were loath to handle a lowly sack until one said, 'Mais c'est du lavande.' At this, they were happy to hug the sack and allow it on to the aeroplane, obviously pleased to be so scented.

London was quite different. This sack caused dismay. When I said what it was the Customs official looked carefully at his list. 'Is it seeds?' he asked. 'Sort of,' I said. This would be cheaper than perfumes, I understood, so finally after bargaining to achieve a low rate of import duty I had the sack hauled into my car and drove back to Kent.

Lavender dolls were becoming big business and they were my introduction to the National Trust. After the Trust was set up they sold souvenirs of their houses, and in 1970 Pat Albeck started to design souvenirs for them, which they used to sell in their entrance halls on benches, since they had no shops. I think Pat was mostly designing souvenir tea towels at which she was brilliant, but we both decided that the National Trust could sell souvenir lavender bags. 'Three Little Maids' – 'The Cook, the Parlourmaid and the Housemaid' made a little set which we sold in a box; they were followed by Beatrix Potter's 'Peter Rabbit, Jemima Puddleduck and Tom Kitten'. Later the National Trust set up shops in their houses organised by Ray Halett, who fitted neat shelves in each house and asked me for goods with a gardening theme, particularly aprons and kneelers. We needed something hard wearing for this and Pat produced a beautiful acorn design which we printed on hessian garden aprons and kneelers. Hessian was too heavy for my girls to cut and stitch in their homes. I understood such work was undertaken in the local prison which they then did satisfactorily for me for several months, stitching hundreds of hessian garden aprons. Fortunately we had them all inspected before we despatched them to the Trust. It was as well we did so, as inside several aprons we found some Force Ten vulgarities written on the hessian. It would have done our reputation no good if a ladylike National Trust customer had found such embarrassing comments inside, or something much worse. Fortunately we were able to edit out the prison humour before it saw the light of day.

Alas one day our supplies from the prison ceased. When I inquired I was told that the Sikh stitcher, who made nearly all our aprons, had gone 'over the wall' and escaped. No one else could make them so well. So it was then I decided to buy some light industrial sewing machines for some of the girls to have in their homes on which to stitch heavy work, and some of them were happy to do this.

Our old stables were getting very, very busy. The goods brought in by the supervisors were tucked singly into plastic bags before being checked against invoices for parcels being sent all over the world. We sent goods to America, to Canada, to South Africa and to many places in Europe, so great care had to be taken to keep up the standards and to check the correct quantities.

So now I had winter work – all the year round work in fact for my dear old fruit pickers. One of them was packing a parcel for South Africa but it was going very slowly. She examined each product meticulously and more times than not she threw it out under the table instead of packing it in the box.

'Please Mrs West, what was wrong with that one?' I asked.

'It had a crooked stitch,' she said as she threw it away. 'Here in Kent we have world wide fame. I'm sending out nothing that is not perfect.'

'We shall have no fame nor work left if you throw everything away,' I said, 'so please don't be quite so fussy.'

I went through all her discards with her and was able to rescue most of them.

I learned later from one of my workers, Margaret Smith, that all my staff called me 'Mother' behind my back, whereas Bill was 'Brigadier'.

It was at about this point that we realised we must find larger premises to work from. We looked round about in Kent, and nearly took on an old mill in the heart of West Malling, but another beautiful old building came on the market about ten miles away in Borough Green. We had to have planning permission for light industrial work and when we moved to this half-timbered old mill we thought it would last us forever, but after some years we had to build a large warehouse alongside, to house all our raw materials.

12

The Tea Cosy Lady

Now I had to learn about business. I had to have agents to sell my goods worldwide, and rent a stand at gift fairs to sell my goods. The Design Centre were very helpful. Early on, they called together a group of us who regularly showed their goods with them in the Haymarket. We were told they thought we were all doing well with our original productions, but knew very little about business practice. Indeed, Mr Blumer would have agreed. The Design Centre Management said they had decided to help us by asking leaders of British Industry to meet us and advise us on our business problems. We suppliers were all ranged along one side of the room, and the industrial magnates on the other, probably embarrassed to be invited. One by one they came over to meet us, to discuss and advise. It was certainly very good of them to do it. The head of ICI, the head of the British BMC, the head of Shell, and other great companies, all came.

The head of Burma Shell was introduced to me – John Raisman. 'Did you live in Delhi as a boy, and were you one of my cubs?' I asked. 'Yes indeed I was,' he said, 'I used to hunt with the Delhi Hounds too.'

He has been a good friend ever since. He is now Chairman of the British Empire Museum, which focuses on the worldwide rule of the British Empire. Bill and I sent each of our books to the Museum, and they sent an lady interviewer, who used to work for the BBC, to gather experiences for their records. She did not seem too interested in me, only recording the fact that I had opened the ball with the Viceroy, but she wanted to hear all about Bill's Indian Cavalry experiences.

'What was your most interesting experience in the Indian Cavalry?' she asked.

'I think probably the parade of four thousand horses at Bolarum in Hyderabad,' he replied. 'We did a walk past, a trot past, and a gallop past. Two hundred and fifty horses in lines, and we had to swing and turn in straight lines at the end of the parade ground.'

'That must have been very difficult,' she said. 'Had you any special rules for swinging two hundred and fifty horses round in a straight line which you were leading?'

'No, not specially,' said Bill. 'Just my natural brilliance.' It was a flippant throwaway, but I couldn't help thinking it was probably true as Bill was indeed a brilliant horseman.

As well as making souvenirs for 'Backing Britain', I thought it would be good to make little presents for children. I looked at books for children and thought Dick Bruna's simple characters were most attractive. The one I really liked was Dick Bruna's teddy bear. So I set off to find him in Holland to ask him if I could use his designs. I got terribly lost in a traffic jam in Utrecht, and when I finally found Dick Bruna, I realised that his teddy bear was virtually a self-portrait. He was a very attractive, round little man. I so enjoyed working with him. His bear motif was used by a racing driving team to bring them luck, and is now a much loved and famous character. Dick Bruna later designed Miffy the rabbit, and I used this character as well on bath wash mitts and little hand towels for children.

By now, business was increasing, and I received a telegram which said 'Understand turnover now only a quarter of a million. Shall we send food parcels? Love Molly and Goff.'

To sell my products, I had to show them at gift fairs. The most important was the one at the National Exhibition Centre at Birmingham. I used to drive to and fro in February, with the snow and slush splashing all over my car – most unpleasant, but I quite enjoyed the shows. I had a major competitor in printed cotton gifts called Sari Fabrics. They always had a large and eye-catching stand. I could only have a much smaller one, and had to do all I could to make it dramatic and attractive. The key was to be able to stop people in their tracks as they walked past, so that they took another look. I had many wonderful customers. Some old friends, and some who were new and whom I liked. I had one French lady who said, 'I have a garden in France – I want to start a little shop but my husband does not like me to spend money.'

'Do you think you could manage two or three hundred pounds?' I asked. 'If so, we'll choose some nice things for you to sell.' This we did, and then she gave me her address as Vaux-le-Vicomte. This was of course the very greatest garden in France – the one which made Louis XIV so envious that he used its designer, Le Nôtre, for designing his gardens at Versailles. The lady who gave me the order, the Contesse de Vogué, went to stay at Chatsworth and told the Duchess she should have some of my things. So I think I did sell a few to the Chatsworth gift shop as a result.

It took me some little while to realise that so many of the creative, clever people who worked in the gift trade were the dramatically inclined. On one occasion I was standing in the aisle when a most elegant figure dressed in pale blue, with waved grey hair, came mincing up the aisle towards me, making sure that everyone in the nearby stands was looking on. He bowed low over my hand and kissed it and said, 'It's the great lady herself. Will she come and join me for a cup of coffee and a chat?' The chat consisted of him telling me all about his lovely gift shop in a select London suburb, and he finally announced that he 'bought all Prince Andrew's pyjamas'. I don't suppose that Prince Andrew knew who bought pyjamas for him, but it was a coup for my friend to say so.

On a later occasion, I was trying on a dress in a cubicle in Liberty's, when someone in the shop called out, 'That's a well-known voice. I must see you and say hello.'

I called back from the cubicle 'Well you can't. I'm in my petticoat.'

The voice replied, 'I don't mind, ducks', and the curtain was flung back, and I was embraced warmly, in my petticoat, by a friend who had been a gift buyer, but was now my agent in New Zealand, and back in the UK on holiday.

At the Birmingham Gift Fair, at the National Exhibition Centre, my chief enjoyment was staying with my friends Johnny Kilmaine and his partner Mike Fisher, who had several other exhibitors staying with them. They lived in sixteenth-century Ravenshaw Hall where they had started an engineering business as manufacturers of whale tankers, for transporting sewage. They kept their work force happy with an assault course. There were twenty-two different challenges around their little lake. They had rope bridges, monkey swings, a netting wall, two long drop ropes to swing across the lake, plus giant lily pads to run across, which wobbled on the water. Failing any of these challenges meant you probably got soaked by falling in the lake. All for fun, as well as for keeping fit. It was a happy team.

Johnny and Mike were gradually restoring Ravenshaw Hall when Bill and I stayed there for the first time. Bill was so cold he made a nightcap for his bald head. Despite this, he refused to stay there again. However, I was a regular guest; some of the others were David Brooksbank, a keen skier, known as Mr Engraved Glass, then Reg Whitehead, known as Mr Plank, who sold shelving, and who reckoned he could sell anything, from left-footed gumboots to out of date calendars. They loved calling me 'Mrs Cuddly Toys', because of my Cuckoobird products. We were all very gloomy over sales in the first few days, but always ended by saying we had had a successful week.

We carried on busily working at Cuckoobird and were happy to provide much local employment. When we were wondering what else to make, the Harrods buyer said they had been asked for a cottage tea cosy: I'd never heard of such a thing. But I cut out and made a cottage shape, with padding for the thatched roof and folded in at the sides to make the end of the thatch. I then unstitched it and laid the pieces out flat, and asked Pat to design a cottage for us. The result was brilliant, and I was most grateful to the Harrods buyer, as the cottage became a best seller, and even now I'm asked for cottage tea cosies from as far away as America. It also caused me to be known as 'the tea cosy lady'.

Eventually, when Bill was eighty years old, still doing all the sums and administration, and I was seventy-two, we thought it was only fair to our workers to retire, in case we let them down through ill health. We sold the business to a Government-sponsored agency who gave work to handicapped people, which I thought was a good idea. They would also keep on many of my workers. They failed to make money and had to sell it again to another firm who had seen our work at a gift fair. They kept on our designers and still sell well. In most National Trust gift shops you can still find goods made by Cuckoobird, probably designed by Pat Albeck, my old friend.

So Bill settled down again to writing books – publishing five in the last twelve years. His first major work had been *Umma More,* published in 1983. This was the name of the ancient stronghold of his family whose Pictish descent had caused his line to inhabit Ireland for 7,000 years before the Celts reached that country. To explain the exploits of his family he had in fact to write the History of Ireland.

When his publisher went out of business he was invited to update *Umma More* to take account of the work then being done for the Peace Process. Bill accurately forecast the result of their negotiations when his book *The Story Of Ireland* was later published in 2000.

His other books were *An Irish Boyhood*, a charming story, followed by *Middle Eastern Approaches*, an account of some of his experiences in Intelligence. His last book, *Soldier of the Raj*, is a very successful account of a Cavalry officer and his regimental soldiering with loyal Indian soldiers as well as of demanding treks in the Himalayas.

I took up my painting again, and decided to paint to help fund mental health, as I had our sad experience of our son's schizophrenia so strongly in mind. I had two friends who were very good painters, one an architect Jean Christopherson, who painted large landscape oils, and another, Jane Mackay, an archaeological draughtsman, who had worked both on and under water, and did little vignettes which were always best sellers. We thought we would have a show in my old garage block, but decided it wasn't large enough; so we asked a local school to house us, which they kindly did. Over the years we have added more and more artists, and then moved to larger premises, and then to Combe Bank School, outside Sevenoaks. We kept our prices low, and only took twenty-five per cent commission for our charities, although galleries have to ask forty per cent. The charities were very grateful, as in the seventeen years since we started, we have given over £136,000 to various mental health charities, a quite surprising result. The private view of the show was developed as a happy evening party for Kent society. A record number of paintings were always sold, in spite of apparently non-stop gossiping. We had the public view on Sundays, to sell what was left over. The National Schizophrenic Society, who now call themselves Re-Think, have always been very helpful at the shows, and so grateful for our contributions.

13
Gardening from Nine to Ninet

My gardening life started when I was eight or nine ye
boarding school at Oldfeld. The art mistress had a small
cottage in the school grounds and part of her garden was divided
into little plots where the pupils could do their own gardening.
There was quite a demand for these plots and I know the boys used
chiefly to love growing vegetables. A large vegetable marrow was a
solid achievement as well as being edible, and a potato or tomato a
triumph.

I suppose I had always loved colour and so I grew nothing but
flowers. I used to get seeds from Woolworth's in highly coloured
packets for which I hoped to get highly coloured results, but this
was optimistic and it was a great day when a large marigold flow-
ered for me to give to the art mistress.

We were allowed to use little packets of chemical fertiliser –
supposed to be magic; a practice which would be frowned on by us
organic gardeners today. I also used to do the watering for my
grandmother, who had a large conservatory, in which she liked to
grow all sorts of plants, and where I tried to grow a few flowers in
pots.

In India at my father's house in Delhi I became really keen on the
large garden. Because of the heat in the summer, we only had an
English-type herbaceous border in the winter, as well as a large
vegetable garden where the *mali* used to grow cauliflowers as big
as soup plates as well as carrots, lettuces and beans. All vegetables
had to be carefully washed in 'pinky-pani'. This was water with
permanganate of potash to compete with possibly disease-ridden
water. Through most of the summer we were able to grow tall
canna lilies in hot colours which were highly decorative. I remember beautiful flowering trees – blue jackaranda as well as orange

and scarlet bougainvilleas on the walls of the bungalow. In Simla, our small garden on the hillside produced plenty of potatoes and other vegetables and we grew roses everywhere – particularly the wonderful yellow climbing Banksia rose which was originally found in Botany Bay in Australia by Sir Joseph Banks.

In Egypt the weather was not helpful to gardening as there were so many *khamsin* sandstorms and we had to garden on the sands of the desert. However the garden was irrigated by water from the Nile which caused the wisteria I mentioned to grow at such high speed beside our bungalow, quickly spreading all over the tin roof.

This was all a prelude to my gardening at our old rectory home in Kent. This garden was basically a very neglected Victorian garden. The house was surrounded by hump-backed Victorian gravel paths with massive dark laurel shrubberies nearby, almost looking into the windows. Bill and I both personally dug up the old gravel paths and used stone paving or grass instead. We dug up all the laurel shrubberies for a bonfire and made wide lawns all around the house. We finally surrounded the garden with yew hedges to be clipped only once a year and planned to be clipped into topiary shapes. As we were still hard up I managed to buy yew seedlings at a shilling each at a Women's Institute plant fair. With these I planted a wide half-moon-shaped hedge in front of the house which we fed with loads of manure from a local stable. The yew seedlings grew well and it was not many years before we had a handsome hedge which could be clipped into large arcs between balustrades of yew topiary, topped by shaped yew balls.

When I started gardening at St Michael's I used to drive to nearby Sissinghurst to study the gardens there. I used to meet and talk with Vita Sackville-West. She was always dressed like a boy in breeches and gaiters with her secateurs tucked into the top of her gaiters. I am sure that she always had in mind that she would have inherited Knole if she had been a boy and not a girl.

We discussed a lot of gardening matters which I found very helpful. She showed me an apple tree that was looking very poorly and asked what I thought. Because I had been learning about fruit I was able to tell her that it had a severe attack of armillaria (honey fungus) and what to do about it.

In another part of the garden her husband Harold Nicolson used to sit on a bench under a tree from where he could survey the borders planted against the walls of the old castle. This reminded me that my father had remembered him as a boy when my father and his brothers and the Nicolson boys used to travel together to Gibraltar for their school holidays. The Nicolsons were on their way to stay with their diplomat father who served in Tangier and Morocco. The Nicolsons were in the charge of a young tutor and my father and his brothers were amused to see how the boys dealt with him. They assured the young man that their father would be most displeased if they were not served with wine at every meal so that they could study the different vintages and learn about wine, even though they were very young. So the tutor sanctioned this step and any other fancies they might invent. My father and his brothers, with no such illusory permission, wondered what would have been their father's intention.

Later on I used to paint watercolours in the gardens of Sissinghurst. I was painting near the end of the old moat when Nigel Nicolson asked me if I would paint his portrait standing in front of his newly-built gazebo. I explained that I was only a landscape painter and had never attempted portraits. Nigel then produced a postcard from his pocket of Mr and Mrs Andrews, a painting by Gainsborough. 'Just like this,' he said, 'with plenty of Kent landscape behind the figures.' In the end I had to have a go and my little picture of Nigel used to hang for years behind all the maps on the walls of the gazebo where he did his writing. I believe that later on he employed a professional portrait painter to do justice to him standing in front of his gazebo. A little beyond my skills.

In the garden at St Michael's I personally moved the wide herbaceous border in front of the hedge five times. I then decided to plant the garden in colours that were happy together. I planted a large curved hot border with warm-coloured foliage to show up against the yew hedge. The foliage included yellow philadelphus aureus, red rhus cotinus, and acer-japonica, a lower planting of bright yellow euphorbia polychroma, yellow marjoram and alchemilla mollis. In between came the highlight of the flowers: in the spring we had tulips in a range of hot colours through reds, oranges and yellows, which made a magnificent display. By this time I was able to buy tulips wholesale and I had 3,000 tulips flowering in this border alone, as well as another 2,000 in white, pink and lavender in other borders. Later the hot bed had red and orange poppies and a mass of later lilies, kniphophia, and crocosmia. Because of the carefully considered colours there were many articles and photographs of our garden in leading garden magazines, as well as many hundreds of visitors who got our details from the *Yellow Book*.

This is what I eventually achieved. The garden took years to create and become established. It also needed gates to open into the field beyond. A local blacksmith produced four wrought-iron gates in designs of 'Spring', 'Summer', 'Autumn', and 'Winter'. They are masterly works of art.

We gave up the croquet lawn in front of the house as it was on a slope and not suitable for skilful play. Our boys loved sport and in the winter they used to toboggan down the hill behind the house or down the slope on our neighbour's field, where they had to be careful not to crash into the frozen stream at the bottom. In the summer, after an attempt to make a one-hole golf course on our hillside, we decided to have a tennis court. So Bill said he would mark out the area and level it himself. Armed with a spade he dug down and down to reach the area to level, and carted off a mountain of soil – most of it heavy clay. This digging, while good exercise, proved too much for him and ended in his having a slipped disc. This was most painful and incapacitating, so eventually we had to pay for a bulldozer to make a level area for a hard tennis court. Bill's was laid up in bed for months with his slipped disc. We got a consultant from King's College Hospital who advised him to sleep with his mattress on a hard board like a door, and to sleep with a hard cushion under his back, which he did. We then got a cable from Bill's cousin, Dr Wellesley Magan in California, inviting us to fly over to his clinic for a 'remedial operation'. We could not afford to do this and many years later when we visited California, Dr Wellesley examined Bill, pronounced that his back had recovered and 'was a fine example of conservative treatment'. At last Bill could walk properly again.

The story of my garden goes on with the addition of my White Border with masses of white roses and anemones, a large romneya, and crambe cordifolia, followed by the elegant white hydrangea, Annabelle, with of course large plantings of various white tulips in their seasons. This border was joined by a wide arch covered in white alba roses (the White Rose of York), beautiful exochorda, 'the Bride' leading to my blue and white bed with a tall pyrus salicifolia, and magnolia, Eddie's White Wonder (an awful name for a lovely thing). The whole bed was surrounded by small blue leafed hostas with pale mauve flowers.

I am afraid I so enjoy my garden I am taking too long talking about it. So I will only say that I also have a lovely large soft pink corner with many different varieties of pink roses on the walls and shrub roses, peonies and pinks in the borders, later lilies with lovely scents where it is a pleasure to sit – if gardeners are ever able to do so.

By the time our sons grew up and George had bought his wonderful 'summer palace' in Ireland to replace the Irish house we had had to sell, I was a very interested gardener. George's house had once belonged to Lady Salisbury's family, the Wyndham-Quinns, before they moved to Adare Castle (now a hotel, I believe). They were a very ancient Irish family and when Mollie was engaged to Lord Cranborne, before he became Lord Salisbury, he introduced his future bride (who was a descendant of Brian Boru, and the High Kings of Ireland) as 'Meet my Bog Girl!'

Mollie Salisbury must now be one of the most famous gardeners in England. At Hatfield she restored the ancient gardens round the old Palace where Queen Elizabeth had been held prisoner, all planted now, with species which grew in Tudor times. Mollie restored and renewed all the gardens at Hatfield after parts of the house had been used as a hospital during the war. Her father was in the Navy and so she spent much of her youth in Ireland, at Castletown Cox, with her grandparents. This is our son George's new home, so she was delighted to be invited to restore the gardens there when so many Irish houses were falling into decay. George asked me to assist as I knew a little about gardens and I was so pleased to be involved in such a marvellous project.

We also had a firm of landscape architects who were working on the fields and forestry. I'm convinced that the head of this firm is a spiritual descendant of 'Capability' Brown. He spoke to me severely as we stood in front of Castletown with its beautiful views of the surrounding mountains.

'You can talk to me as long as you like,' he said, 'but you won't change my opinion. You should have the fields coming up to the house.'

'I only said that I don't think my son George will want cows under his drawing room windows,' was my reply.

George did *not* want cows! He much preferred Mollie Salisbury's new suggestions for flower parterres below the house. There had originally been some green box parterres at the sides which were a lovely pattern but which Mollie said were in the wrong position architecturally. So we moved both these box parterres twelve feet to become central to the fine arcades in front of the house. We were told the box would never survive being dug up and moved, but it did. In addition, to fill the space Mollie designed two green parterres at each end with George and his wife Wendy's initials in clipped box.

That was only the start of parterres. Mollie drew on some ancient patterns and produced some beautiful designs for flower-filled box parterres in front of the house. The parterres were most elegant and were planned to be filled with flowers in purple, pale blue, mauve and cream from April to September. I told the gardeners that this was a 'horticultural high jump' as it was immensely difficult to maintain in top condition for so long. The fact that they achieved it is a great tribute to their skill. We then had a visit from the Irish Genealogical Society. One of them was an architect. He looked down on the parterres as he stood beside me on the balcony.

'I've designed many French châteaux and their parterres,' he said 'and these parterres are quite wrong. They should be level box hedges with coloured gravel or coloured foliage between parterres with no plants showing above the hedges.'

'I know that is the classical French idea,' I said, 'but do they have charm?'

'Oh no,' he said, 'they're not supposed to have charm.'

I thought Mollie Salisbury's designs, with a delicate silhouette of different flowers above the box, had immense charm.

'I think that these flower parterres are Lady Salisbury's great contribution to gardening,' I said.

So we agreed to differ.

All who visit Castletown now find these parterres, so beautifully clipped into shapes by the gardeners, a delight. In fact a delegation from the New York Botanic Gardens wrote to Mollie to say they thought the Castleton gardens were the best and most original they had seen in Ireland (chiefly because of her parterres, I'm sure). Mollie does the patterns and I do my best to support her with the colours. No reds, oranges, strong pinks or yellows are allowed and it is extremely satisfying to keep it all in balance. To do all this is any gardener's dream. I have so enjoyed not only the results but the enormous pleasure of working with Mollie.

My own contribution to the gardens in Ireland has been the blue garden. The start of this came from an inspiration I had in Kashmir when I was a girl.

Under the snow-covered mountains, on a snowy alp, was the house of a forest officer I knew. The track to it ran along the edge of a tall pine forest. Between the pines and the track grew a very wide border of blue Himalayan poppies (meconopsis), a fantastic sight. The blue against the pines below the snowy mountains was a dream that stayed with me for years.

So in Ireland I started a wide meconopsis border, backed by dark yews and pines, beside the lake. Beyond this is a small wooden bridge, stained pale blue above a bank covered in blue flowers, hydrangeas, agapanthus, iris sibirica and ceanothus. The stream below is edged with a wide border of Japanese iris (ensata), their blues and purples reflected, as well as iris laevigata growing in profusion in the water. From a circular blue-stained bench beneath a willow tree you can get glimpses of my blue Himalayan poppies as well as of the shining silver lake, the home of the white swans. The swans like to visit the ensata garden with their cygnets and occasionally choose to walk, sit and nest among the Japanese iris. We have to discourage this, however decorative they look.

14
The Time of Our Life

In 1992 we visited India at the invitation of Bill's old Indian Cavalry regiment, Hodson's Horse, who gave us a marvellous ten days in Nabha near Patiala. It happened that the last day there was also the occasion of our wedding anniversary and one of their officers, Jack Sawhney, invited us to return to Delhi, where we were married, for any other anniversary that we chose.

Our son George said, 'Millennium Year, your Diamond Wedding.' So he, his wife Wendy, Bill and I set off for India on Monday 27 November 2000, to be met at Delhi airport by Major Vivek Gupta from Hodson's Horse and two Indian officers. We stayed at the Imperial Hotel, where I had attended so many dances in the past. Most of the staff made a point of congratulating us on our sixty years of marriage.

We reminded ourselves of historic Delhi. George and Wendy visited the Willingdon nursing home where George was born and later we got special permission to visit my father's old house where we had lived for about ten years. This was 9 Race Course Road. The Prime Minister now lives in No. 7 Race Course Road next door, and uses all the houses in this short road as his personal offices.

The 'Hodson's family' in Delhi had very kindly invited us to dine in the Sabre Officers' Mess of the Indian Armoured Brigade. These were nearly all very senior officers who had moved on from the regiment to higher command or were now retired. Our hosts were General Gurinder (Guri) Singh and his wife. General Vohra and my dear old friend Mrs Vohra, together with General Malik, General Narindar Singh and Colonel Bhatt. The latter had the distinction of being the most decorated officer. His wife said he had had four tanks shot from under him, and had somehow escaped. There were many other old friends there too.

The new Mess was magnificent. I have never seen a finer collection of silver – enormous silver cups and trophies, several two or three feet high, an elegant silver replica of a tank and scores of photographs and paintings. There was a gathering of about sixty officers and their wives to meet us, and one or two of the younger ones rather threw Bill by wanting him to identify officers in a photograph of the 1880s! He explained that he had been born in 1908. We were all standing round having drinks when in marched in the mess *duffadar* – he seemed to be seven feet tall with a magnificent turban, huge gold waistband and high boots. He looked like something straight out of Hollywood. In ringing tones he announced to General Gurinder 'Khana tyar huzzoor', ('Food is ready, sir' in Hindi) – an ancient custom – and then marched out again.

As the Mess dining room was not large enough to seat all of us, all the white heads and grey beards were seated at small tables and the younger people walked round chatting. I sat next to General Narindar Singh. We all helped ourselves to an elegant buffet, masterminded by an officer's wife. She and I and Mrs Bhatt talked of how we enjoyed cooking. All the officers' wives now do their own cooking and housework but they do have a batman to take care of their husband's uniform and very occasional help in the house and garden. Most of them like to have jobs as well, and teaching fits well into a life where they have to be on the move. Vivek Gupta's wife was a clothes designer, Mrs Gurindar Singh a lawyer.

At the end of supper we withdrew to the drawing room where General Gurinder presented us with a silver frame from the Hodson's officers in Delhi to hold a photograph of our visit, with our names inscribed, to mark the occasion.

Thursday was our anniversary and it was the greatest pleasure that our son James was also able to be with us. His superiors at Mother Teresa's Missionaries of Charity very kindly posted him to one of their establishments for handicapped children near Delhi, so that he could join us. We all had lunch at the hotel before going on to the Cathedral Church in New Delhi, where we had been married at the same time sixty years before. There we had an unexpected reception. Colonel Anil Bhatt of the Regiment had retired and was now working in public relations, and it must have been due to him that we were greeted by an increasing throng of photographers and reporters all popping flashes at us. Some twenty-five of them surged up the aisle in front of us and then ranged themselves in front of our pew, continually scrambling for places as we tried to attend to the service and the hymns we had chosen.

It was hard to see the vicar, the Revd Colin Theodore, a very nice warm man, above the milling photographers in front of us. I thought they should never have been allowed in. There were no Christians in Hodson's Horse so Colonel Dusty Sen, a 19th Lancer and a Christian, read the first lesson. James was unexpectedly invited to read the second and George was asked to give an impromptu address. They both did well. We received a quiet bless-ing on our marriage from the vicar and walked out with the media scrum reversing in front of us. There were more outside, and finally loud demands for Bill to give me a kiss, with which he had to oblige six times for the cameras. He said that after a lifetime in the Secu-rity Service during which he had kept a very low profile, it was a shock to be the centre of all this media attention. Photographs and articles appeared in fifteen leading Indian newspapers the next day.

We and our guests then thankfully withdrew to the Imperial Hotel where George and Wendy had arranged a reception in the garden, but again we had more interviews. The hotel had given us a large two-tiered cake which Bill and I cut with a sword while cham-pagne glasses were filled. Bill then made a speech.

We left Delhi by the 6 am 'Shatabdi Express' the next day to visit Hodson's Horse, now known as Four Horse, and mechanised, at Babina. The 'Shatabdi Express' was an air-conditioned coach with reclining seats – a big advance from travelling in our day. We were met by Colonel Ajai Shukla with a fleet of small regimental cars – 'Brigadier Magan CBE' printed on ours. Many of the senior officers had also come to celebrate Cambrai Day the following day, commemorating the battle where the regiment had distinguished itself in 1914. At the start of the First World War Hodson's and their horses had travelled from India to France in three months – timing that would challenge an armoured corps today.

Bill was taken off separately to visit the troops whom he found very smart and impressive. Wendy and I had asked to see the families, so we shook hands with about fifty wives and met the children who were not in school. We also admired and bought handicrafts made by Army wives.

We ladies were then given two rather martial treats. We were invited to climb on to one of two huge Russian tanks on the parade ground – they were old models still serviceable and used by the Indian armoured corps. They were hard to mount in fancy shoes and I found it quite hard not to fall down the well below me in which a Sikh soldier was driving us very gently to make sure we did not fall off. Later George had a ride and they drove him very fast. We were then taken pistol-shooting and shown how to point our guns at the enemy. Wendy and I both succeeded in hitting the wooden target three times out of four, quite creditable, and George managed eight out of eight.

In the meantime Bill had been taken round the lines and blessed by both a Sikh and a Hindu priest. He had a red thong tied round his wrist and an orange scarf round his shoulders, as well as two holy books, one of them the Gita. Colonel Ajai Shukla then gave us a buffet lunch in the regimental Mess which he preceded with a warm welcoming speech. The Indian officers presented us with a banner with regimental crests embroidered on it by their wives in gold and silver thread – it now hangs on show in our hall. My painting of Hodson's Gloucestershire home and Bill's of the silver quarterguard bell both hang in the Mess. We gave them a heavy crystal vase with a diamond cut pattern, and a large album of photographs.

Next we went to Agra. On the way there a Minister in the Government who represented the Indian minority group called the Rainbow Coalition boarded the train and came to greet us. He told us he had seen our photographs in the press and wished to congratulate us. On arrival at Agra we were met by the Prime Minister of Agra who did the same.

At the ancient fort of Fatehpore Sikri – more marvellous Mogul architecture – we were accosted by a tall Indian who informed us he was a Pathan from the North West. His Persian wife and Bill exchanged some greetings in Persian in response to her request to have our photograph (she had also seen us in the newspapers). They were the first of many who also congratulated us. We became quite a tourist attraction.

After Agra we were driven to Jaipur across the endless plains of India. Little cultivated fields for miles, all irrigated, often from wells where the buffaloes walked round and round and the waterwheels dropped water from round terracotta pots – *chattis* – which emptied into water channels and each field was irrigated in turn.

Jaipur was still a wonderful city. The last maharajah still lived in the top apartments of his City Palace from where he used to be able to look down on to dancing ladies in the courtyard below. For the visit of the Prince of Wales the whole city had been ordered to be painted pink. Most of it still remained pink and looked very good. Our guide took us to a back alley which we should never have found on our own, where there worked some of the finest cutters of precious stones in the world. The water into which the powder from the cut stones fell was used for miniature painting.

On our return to Delhi at Gurgaon we called on our son James's Deepashram, Mother Teresa's establishment there, to which he had been posted. He took us to a large building topped by an enormous cross. This had all been built by Mother Teresa's Missionaries of Charity. Brother Matthew who had been there from the outset, when it was a bare patch of ground, met us with most of the fifty-five handicapped children who had been rescued by the Charity after having been abandoned. They sang us a song of welcome which was most touching as so many were pathetic sights. They were given much free help – physiotherapy, medication, dentistry, occupational therapy and some teaching – so that some at least could be fitted eventually to hold their own in the world outside. James said there was quite considerable anti-Christian feeling so they had to exercise great care in their dealings. They never tried to change the religion of the children, but had not gone so far as to invite Hindu priests to visit them. James said they were about to open yet another centre in Kerala in South India and he was likely to be sent there. This was a relief to me as it was a beautiful place and a much better climate.

We took James to have supper with us on the edge of the airport at the Radisson Hotel. As we approached I remarked on the opulence of the illuminated frontage and James said 'If you find this a bit much, you can imagine how I feel!' He had been living his life with the poorest of the poor for twelve years.

Five years after George had given us the time of our life by flying us first class to India for our diamond wedding, he decided to fulfil a dream of his own. He had always wanted to visit Istanbul, and decided to take his family there to celebrate his sixtieth birthday. I later received this note, written on the eve of his birthday.

Dear Mother,
    Inveigled by my children away from the 'flesh pots' of the Ottoman Empire, I find myself, on the eve of my sixtieth birthday, swooning in the torrid steams of this Historic Haman, a three hundred year old torture chamber! Then I am pummelled to within an inch of my life by an elderly hairy Turk in a loincloth. Other than myself, everyone else seems to find all of this hilariously entertaining. As I enter the geriatric zone, familial respect seems to be waning.

Although his lifelong dream seems to have included this small nightmare, I do not think the results were too serious. He dined with us on his return and, on close inspection, there appeared to be no diminution of his significant silhouette and I feel confident that he will continue to prosper.

Envoi

Looking back at my early life – all part of a bygone era – I think I have been most fortunate. I recall the influence on my young imagination of my romantic Highland ancestry and sedate Quaker forebears. I used to love hearing of my parents' early adventurous life in India. I later enjoyed travels to far places in Africa and all over India.

My chief good fortune has been my marriage to Bill, my 'soldier of the Raj'. His splendid sense of humour has meant we have been able to laugh together nearly every day. It has also been a profound satisfaction to be able to support him in his distinguished career in the Security Service (MI5). This office, whose motto on their coat of arms is 'Regnum Defende' ('Defend the Realm'), has always impressed me as being both able and principled. Not in it for reward (they don't get it!) or honours, they work behind closed doors to the highest standards of efficiency, for our protection. I so much appreciate having been invited to become an honorary member of the Services Society for former members of staff.

My next piece of good fortune must be my having been born into the British Empire at its zenith and to have been part of it in my youth. I know from personal experience the standards of integrity and high endeavour which drove its servants, and I think that at least those qualities should be remembered at a time when history tends to frown on past imperial power.

I am so grateful for the friends I have had fun with, the loyalty of the workers in my many ventures and having been able to paint, garden and work with some success. But my family is my greatest joy – all so good to me, with a generation of grandchildren now making their mark and Bill, at nearly 100, still a gallant officer in spite of his frail health and advanced years. I salute him.

[123]

Index